In Turbulent Waters

J. Lambert St Rose

To: Diane

8/12/2014

authorHOUSE®

AuthorHouse™ LLC
1663 Liberty Drive
Bloomington, IN 47403
www.authorhouse.com
Phone: 1-800-839-8640

Published by AuthorHouse 09/03/2014

ISBN: 978-1-4969-3784-1 (sc)
ISBN: 978-1-4969-3783-4 (hc)
ISBN: 978-1-4969-3785-8 (e)

Library of Congress Control Number: 2014915742

For permission contact:
J. Lambert St. Rose
P.O. Box 726, Castries, St. Lucia
Email: *lambert_st@yahoo.com*
Telephone 758 451 8179

Cover design: Paul Krone
Sketches: Gordon Jean Baptiste

Scripture quotations and citations are from the Jerusalem Bible, copyright © 1966 by Darton, Longman, & Todd Ltd and Doubleday and Company Inc. London, With permission.
Text and citations from CTS publications are used with permission.

Contents

Dedicated to:

Gina

Harria

&

Evita

Your struggle has been the hope of my salvation!

Two thousand years and counting,
still, there is no panacea for the Barabbas Syndrome
– villains are given reprieve, innocent men, women and children
are still victims of the crowd's demands.
The Caesars must be appeased and the lambs will be sacrificed.
The just will be condemned, the villains will
enjoy their underserved freedom.

J. Lambert St. Rose

Acknowledgements

Gina, Harria and Evita are the inspiration for this book. Gina was born into a family of witches, her destiny as a witch was written long before she was born. However her friends, Harria and Evita were recruits into that same cult. The three of them shared something in common – a heart and gut-wrenching desire to extricate themselves from Satanism and give their lives to the Lord, which was no easy task.

They endured many assaults and many brushes with death but, they survived to tell their story. Theirs was the mother of all exorcisms. At the end they commissioned Fr. Laport: "Please write this story that other young people may never venture out to swim in the same pool with Satanists."

Thanks for the unique faith and unfailing resilience of a backup prayer team, so loyal to the cause of Gina, Harria, Evita and Fr. Laport; they generously sacrificed their time and effort to beseech the Lord on their behalf throughout the counselling sessions and the rite of exorcism.

To my editors Loyola Devaux and the many others who, because of the fear-provoking nature of the literature opted to remain anonymous and to keep their contribution the same. To my critics, Louvette Louisy and Everistus Jn Marie, I express my most heartfelt and sincere thanks.

Last, but not least, to God my eternal thanks and praise.

Preface

Producing a book is a very arduous task for many reasons. Life presents such a wide variety of experiences which leave their indelible marks on us physically, mentally, emotionally, socially, educationally and spiritually. As we grow older and reminisce on these numerous challenging chapters in our lives, many individuals yearn to share some of the happenings of their lives with others. On the other hand, some writers possess great creative imaginations which attract readers who enjoy intrigue, cyberspace and the unimaginable. Sometimes the factual and the fiction are meshed together to reach wider audiences.

In the case of the author of this book, it is often difficult to decide which is which, as sometimes the various stories and circumstances presented are seemingly so unbelievable. Nevertheless the author has tread where many fear to go - the occult, demonic, Satanic and sadistic areas of human persons who have become worshippers of such ludicrous 'spirits' and cults. Very few people would have the stamina and courage to stand up to hidden realities that exist side by side in our so called 'Christian Society'. We adopt the attitude that, "if I can't see it, I don't know about it, I can't believe it and therefore it cannot really exist. It is merely imagination, fabrication and speculations." However, the author has lived through the agonies of many individuals whose lives have been devastated by their sojourns with the occult, demons, Satan, etc.

The task of trying to release such people from the clutches of the devil is an extremely difficult, emotional and trying experience which invariably can wear you down physically as well as spiritually, if you are not careful and deeply rooted in your faith and belief in Jesus Christ.

The author of this book has spared no effort in rallying and responding to the needs of many 'lost souls' who have finally been relieved and saved from the intricate clutches of the 'demonic'.

The catharsis of the author is meant to make us aware of the realities that exist around us. We must all be knowledgeable and prepared to resist any temptations to dabble with the occult. Indeed the devil never rests! Without a doubt this is a book with a difference!

LOYOLA DEVAUX

Foreword

*I*nsipid Salt or *Children of Esau* could have been a more appropriate title for this tablet novel instead of *In Turbulent waters*. 'Why *Insipid Salt*'? Because evil is baseless and it is worth trampling underfoot. 'Why *Children of Esau*'? Because the partakers of evil are by nature tricksters, killers, hunters and notorious vagabonds in search of divine clothes, powerful skills and cherished property all at the expense of their birthright.

However, the author settled for the title *In Turbulent Waters* because he is better able to identify with the Prophet Jonah *en route* to Nineveh and beyond. Besides, the title *In Turbulent Waters* is best able to capture and articulate the consequences of cultural, traditional and spiritual dislocation. Their victims are squanderers and vagabonds, prodigals only if there is some hope of metanoia.

Squanderers of virtues, vagabonds of grace such are the people who have made darkness their preferential option in opposition to living in the Way, the Light and the Truth. Such are the men and women of yesteryear, today and tomorrow, who have formed and will continue to form alliances with Baphomet in hot pursuit of transient favours: bread, power and glory at any cost. In the abundance of water the fool dies of thirst. Fools contaminate their own reservoirs for short-term gains at the expense of the long-term good. The same applies to those who choose to be servants of Baphomet instead of the Way, the Truth and the Light. They exchange eternal glory for eternal damnation. The end result: they are prodigals of their own doing. For them misery awaits unless metanoia transcends their minds and helps them re-establish an alliance with the Transcendent One. Otherwise pigs' husks may be their last meal and the sties, their final abode.

In the absence of virtues, lust, deception and vindictiveness are never too far from home. Honesty and integrity are easily compromised. Intrigue, trickery, fabrication, bribery, prejudice and injustice are commonplace for persons who find it opportune to satisfy their immeasurable lust and greed. The occult is readily embraced. Faith is compromised. Grace is wasted and human dignity is depleted. Duplicity in religious outlook is the norm rather than its abhorrence renounced at baptism and at the Easter celebrations.

Satisfaction at any cost is, by preference, the motto of such persons. Their victims are unsuspecting innocent individuals who are like raw flesh set before wild hungry beasts. Institutions of justice hijacked by persons of the same ilk aid and abet persons in their crimes even to the point of defeating goodness itself. That too comes at a cost either in cash or in kind, even though it may be at the cost of a human soul, provided material yield is the name of the game. They are often oblivious to the Christocentic maxim, "What shall it profit a man if he gains the whole world and suffers the loss of his own soul?"

Profiteering is an infectious disease. It is easily transmitted to persons sufficiently gullible to believe that bread, power and glory are the only panacea that will restore their inherently disordered self-esteem and character. Often they do not even realize that they are squanderers of virtues and vagabonds of grace. Why? Because they believe only in the tangibles as opposed to faith, grace and the Spirit, faith for them is elusive. In the tangibles, they believe they will find a quick-fix and an expedient ladder to immediate success and achievement in all of life's goals. Life and living are not defined for them by who they are from within but rather by what they own and what they represent in the eyes of the world. Even if the above are earned by means of deception, demonic interventions and the life and well-being of others, they are ambitious only for their material success and the achievement of a social status, bereft as it may of any ethical or spiritual aptitude.

Such persons can also be reckoned vagabonds of culture and squanderers of tradition, victims of cultural dislocation not withstanding whichever level they may occupy in the social stratum. These are the men and women who have radically departed from the objectives of *Listwa* Time: the perpetuation of a holistic genuine human growth and development and the avoidance of evil at all cost.

Humankind has come of age. Philosophers, theologians, sociologists and the like tout it in our ears all the while. In the twenty-first century we speak of the digital age. Therefore, in some measures: "we have come of age". That is if, and only if, this notion of "age" is narrowly interpreted within the narrow confines of the word "civilized" or "industrialized." Civilization and industrialization are more than just about social behaviour and social acceptance and the creation of industries, markets and the like. They are processes through which people are taught philosophical, spiritual or Christian virtues for life in this world and life in the world to come. In other words, it does not limit itself only to the mundane things of life.

There are two dimensions to civilization and industrialization: the social and the spiritual dimension. One must not take precedence over the other. Both are intertwined. Together, they empower people and prepare them for a more holistic way of life. Simultaneously, they prepare people to behave and live in a more human, friendlier context, in a manner that would judge thereafter every individual worthy of his or her humanity. Civilization prepares people for a healthy industrialized society so that business will grow, develop and be sustained in an atmosphere of justice, peace and freedom guided by a healthy and genuine conscience and inspired by the Creator and the principles of natural law.

A truly civilized person is one who possesses a genuine soul, a social and moral conscience. A fully integrated person is a wholesome citizen who is in every sense of the word "moral" with the notable absence of "immoral". Such an individual is capable of finding accommodation within all human cultures and having the ability to adapt to everything good with the deliberate intention of rejecting evil under all conditions. This includes as well, all forms of pretence and disguise of apparent goodness worn as a mask where evil lurks deep within.

Listwa Time, therefore can best be defined as a popular anthropological and enculturation tool invented by the ancestors for easy transmission of culture and tradition. The Soirees were the classrooms where this tool was most effective. It was there that the children of Jacob, with a flair for intellectual stimulus, inherited their rights while the children of Esau, with scant regard for such stimulus, in preference for a life of hunting, killing, divine clothes and cherished property, sold his birthright. Like Esau, many in the Diaspora, in the forest of colonialism, disregarded the lessons taught at *Listwa* Time. The end result: they have sold their souls and desecrated the traditions of the elders and have consequently lost their birthright. They are now strangers in their own souls.

Colonialism taught those living in the Diaspora that many aspects of Afrocentric traditions were superstitions. Yes, there were superstitious beliefs handed down from generation to generation and still are. However, it was the deliberate intention of the ancestors that, through the medium of *Listwa*, the youth were taught to distinguish between good and evil and on all accounts to avoid evil since its effects are dehumanizing. Goodness for the ancestors was never optional. Goodness was, and still is, the preferred option to evil.

Sadly, however, the occult has persisted throughout our history. In more recent times, it has been institutionalized: witches and wizards have infiltrated every institution in our society. Not one is exempt. Not even the churches are exempted. Religion in most instances is a farce. Some Christians and demons share a soul and many at death, are eulogized as saints, while fellow witches and wizards sit and listen with calm indifference in the presence of the Sacred One before whom such lies are lavishly and shamelessly proclaimed.

A Rastafarian in Joseph Owen's book: *Dread, The Rastafarians of Jamaica,* reacted strongly to the statement that his mother was a good woman since she attended daily Mass. He immediately corrected the priest by saying: "Even if she is my mother, do not call anyone good just because he or she is a churchgoer. You can never tell what is in the heart of the other person." He added, "Especially when you do not live under the same roof with that person."

What is this? Isn't it an unacceptable form of syncretism which contributes nothing to anyone or any institution, other than dysfunctional societies and churches and by extension, a dysfunctional world? It is against this background, according to the author that *In Turbulent Waters* has come into being.

Introduction

In Turbulent Waters is a sad but true story of some squanderers of culture and vagabonds of tradition. These prodigals, today, are the squanderers of virtues and vagabonds of grace plaguing Helen Island in their alliance with Baphomet and the blood and human sacrifices offered up to him – a subculture which a young native priest thought all along was just mere myths, legends and fairytales, stories, which he thought were concocted by the elders during their *soirees* to intimidate young minds and keep them housebound after sunset. Little did the young priest in his early childhood and teenage years understand that this subculture do exists. This subculture creates dysfunctional beings. In the past, it has contributed to the demise of many and so it is dangerous territory for one to venture into.

However, very early in his public priestly ministry, the young naïve priest received a wake-up call: reality came home and confronted him to his face. That initial encounter determined the rest of his priestly ministry. He was like Jonah sent to Nineveh but while Jonah's mission to Nineveh lasted only forty days his seems to be a lifetime assignment. The assignments sometimes came with shocking revelations and with churning effects on the stomach; sometimes too much to digest, too much to stomach.

In Turbulent Waters is an attempt to bring out the gravity of the situation and the impact of cultic activities in Helen Island. It also points out the drastic and damaging toll cultic activities have taken on the lives of individuals and some communities as well. Despite the fact that Helen Island is considered a Christian nation, Baphomet wields a heavy hand in many national decisions, supported and encouraged by those considered as highly civilized persons. Witches and wizards are in no shortage in Helen Island.

The names of places and persons *In Turbulent Waters* are all fictional for the sole purpose of protecting the identity of persons. Many have passed from this world and the author prays for the repose of their souls. Still some linger and squirm in their misery because of their stubborn reluctance to embrace conversion. Others are still busy recruiting members into the cults while the members who dare to make their exit, live in perpetual torment with the threat of death hovering over their heads. The author prays for their conversion. His prayers and his heart go out to Julienne, Carla, Gina, Harria and Evita and pray that God will one day grant them the fullness of redemption and deliverance.

In Turbulent Waters, is an admonition for this generation and for future generations to do all within their power to make goodness and righteousness their preferred option and avoid evil at all cost – in other words, be living examples of virtue. Be custodians of grace; be fortifications of culture; be custodians of tradition. Uphold the honour and integrity of our ancestral spirits befitting of our culture, our tradition, our faith and our belief as Christ's bearers. If all else fails, remember we are bearers of our ancestral spirits, once consecrated in Christ Jesus, the image and likeness of God.

Chapter One

Listwa Time
(It's Story Time)

Until the latter half of the twentieth century when television was only just a name, storytelling was quite instrumental as family entertainment and the enculturation of the youth. The youth, in the simplicity of their minds, translated everything they had heard as old wives' tales, myths and legends. James Laport was no exception to that rule. Never in his wildest dreams did he think that one day these same old wives' tales, myths and legends would come right back to determine his ministerial and pastoral contribution to his country.

James Laport grew up on the outskirts of Félicitéville. He had the normal curriculum vitae of all other boys of his age in his neighbourhood: home, school, house chores and church on weekends and holy days of obligation. His mother, was a *Poto Légliz;* his father, a seasonal Catholic who visited the church on occasions such as baptisms, weddings and funerals. Converted by age, more than by conviction, he became a regular Catholic before his last exit from this life. Sometimes on a Sunday afternoon, his deceased aunt, God rest her soul, picked up as many of his brothers and sisters as her derelict Land Rover accommodated and took them for a swim or on an island tour. That was a real treat. The echo of the rattling engine and the banging sound of the loose aluminum body parts of the old Land Rover still resonate in James' mind. But who cares? In those days that was a real luxury. Very few people were able to own even a derelict vehicle and very few had the privilege of being driven to the beach.

His family was itself a football team: fourteen siblings. He never needed other friends to play with. Still, quite a number of the children from the neighbourhood gathered at his family home and joined the group in whatever was on the agenda that day. Whatever meals his mother prepared always multiplied of their own accord to meet the hunger of all the kids who invaded the home for the day, and there were still leftovers.

In his early childhood, television was just a name. All James knew of it was through pictures in books or magazines. The family's nocturnal entertainment included games among siblings and storytelling. The elderly members of the family or of the community reminisced over the past.

Often, they were the same stories but with a different twist: Tim Tim, *Konpè Lapen, Konpè Tig, Bèf Louwa,* ghosts, spirits, *lajables, jan gajé,* Black Magic (sex molesters, men transformed into creatures equipped with extended genitals entered people's homes through keyholes). Their only objective was to molest people's wives and daughters. Their counterparts were called White Magic (women who molested men and young boys in their sleep). Such were the stories or *Listwa* which captivated and gripped the attention of the children at that time. Everyone was always wrapped into the claws of the story teller. Of particular interest too were the methods employed to trap those unwanted demonic intruders and assailants, and how they were brought to their knees when captured. They wept; they mourned; they pleaded with their captors for mercy and release before sunrise. The process of transformation from creature back to human was irreversible after sunrise. In those days, there were numerous stories about persons who were captured while on their nocturnal activities and were subsequently hospitalized, only to be public spectacles. Death was gracious enough to rescue them from public mockery.

Tradition has it that: a hag, as part of the required preparation for transformation from human to creature, peeled off her skin, wrapped it neatly and placed it under a mortar. She then transformed into a goat and wandered away into the dark. A man monitored her closely from the nearby bushes. As soon as she wandered into the dark, he crept out of hiding, and pickled the skin with a pungent peppery concoction, and then he folded the skin and replaced it under the same mortar. He then returned to his hiding place and continued his night vigil until her return in the wee hours of the morning. Hastily, she refitted into her skin. Her swift actions were followed by a spontaneous tap-dance to lyrics and rhythm of a Creole rap composed on the spur of the moment: *Tiyam pa bwilam sé métam ki bwilam* (removal was painless, the refitting is hell). Each time this story was told the children in the audience roared with laughter. Their overstretched imaginations made them dance and twitch to imitate the hag in her hour of irreversible distress.

Inclusive in the nights' agenda was the constant talk of older men who abducted children for child-sacrifice to demons in exchange for special favours. For James, all such stories were myths and legends, although sometimes there were nuances of truth in what was narrated. James took it all with a grain of salt. The stories were both hilarious and frightening all at once. Nevertheless some events, related to such stories were engraved in the psyche of those who heard them.

The Witch Next Door

It was a night James would always remember. The night was pregnant with silence. Had a pin dropped, its echo would have travelled a thousand miles away. There were no tremors, no strong winds, no heavy rains, and no floods. Tranquility was king of the night. That was until about three o' clock in the morning. Suddenly, there was a loud crashing sound. It was the neighbour's house. For no apparent reason it fell off its pillars. Sofa was the only eyewitness to the crash.

Sofa was an elderly cousin, who lived with the Laport family for most of his senior years. For as long as he lived with the Laport family, he had held strong suspicions about an elderly Protestant woman who lived a stone's throw across the road from the Laport family. Each morning Sofa greeted the family with his usual refrain while pointing in the direction of the neighbour's house: "That woman is a witch." He spoke with absolute authority on the matter. To be certain that he was understood, he repeated himself in Creole: "*Mwen ka di zòt fanm sala ka gajé*".

In the wake of the crash, Mr. Laport, James' father, made a dash for the door. His mind was set on the scene of the accident. Sofa accosted him. "Stop!" he said. "Do not bring that woman and her children into your home. You will be taking a big risk." Mr. Laport was befuddled for a minute. "What risk?" Mr. Laport barked back at Sofa. Determined as he was to stop Mr. Laport, Sofa took two steps closer, pointed his index finger into Mr. Laport's face and shouted at the top of his voice, "Do not shelter this woman in your home." He stopped as if to muster some courage, and then added, "She's fully responsible for the destruction of her home." The more Mr. Laport tried to ignore Sofa, the more he protested. "I saw her with my own eyes. She landed on top of her house in the form of a huge bird." As usual Mr. Laport would not listen. He shouted back at Sofa, "You are both drunk and mad."

Sofa was so irate that he was prepared to rip his heart out of his chest as proof. The poor man was a 'rum bug.' No matter how sober he was, he was still considered a drunk. In spite of his protest, Mr. Laport did the contrary.

The elderly woman and her grandchildren were all given shelter by the Laport family for almost a week before the house was rebuilt. For Sofa that was a travesty against God himself. As far as he was concerned, Mr. Laport had compromised the integrity of the Laport's sanctuary. He vowed to himself that he would expose the charade put up by the neighbour. In his own words, this Protestant woman was no more than 'A witch in the garments of a saint.' He looked for an opportunity to expose her duplicity.

Sofa boozed himself religiously every day. He left home punctually at seven o' clock every morning. By four o'clock in the afternoon he was home, and had lunch and supper all at once. By six o'clock in the evening he was sound asleep. Sometimes by ten or eleven o'clock in the night, Sofa was fully awake until daybreak. Like a dutiful sentinel, he sat up at his favourite window and kept watch through the night.

He was the self-appointed family sentinel. He had a panoramic view from his position of command. The window overlooked the said neighbour's house. By the time he woke up to assume his night watch, the effects of the alcohol had evaporated. Usually he was sober up until his return to the city for his first shot. Despite all Sofa's sleepless nights, his panoramic view and his sobriety, the family held strong reservations about his judgement. Poor man, all his efforts were spent in vain.

Everyone in the family argued the woman was a Protestant Christian. Protestants were 'good' people. It almost sounded as if Protestants were *de facto* better Christians than Catholics. That made Sofa really angry. One thing he took great pride in was that he was born on Palm Sunday. The day on which he was born made him blessed and protected. Regardless of the date and month on which the feast fell, that was his birthday. Sofa vowed: as God made Moses, his effort would not go in vain. He was determined to get even with the woman.

After a day or two the neighbours got together, rebuilt the house and reinstated the family. A few weeks later the old hag showed no mercy, no compassion on her little eight year old grandson who had stolen a quarter from her purse. She plunged his tiny hand into a pot of boiling rice and kept it there till it was thoroughly cooked. Her latest action enraged Sofa. This time he was more determined than ever to confront her. However, when he was sober, he didn't have the courage to confront the old hag without an excuse.

One evening Sofa was fully inebriated. Under the influence of his favourite White Rum, all his inhibitions were gone. That evening, on his way home, Sofa stood at the door of the old hag where he openly and freely discharged the full weight of his conscience at her. He disclosed everything he knew and had seen over the years. Everything he remembered he put into the public domain. He told her exactly what he had seen the night her house collapsed. He also told her how much he had watched her activities over the years. When he completed his confrontation with her, Sofa was more sober than a teetotaller. He stood tall. He beat his chest like Tarzan. Then he shouted out loud, "You old devil! Everybody will know who you are now." Next morning the hag and all her grandchildren were gone like the wind. They left the community.

A Haunted House

Meanwhile, just a quarter mile away from the Laport's home, another story was developing. A family home in the neighbourhood was under siege. It was said that the family's home had been taken over by a band of spirits. Night and day the family was physically beaten. Their clothes were mere threads hanging on their bodies. Boulders were repeatedly hurled at their home. Yet there was never ever anyone in sight. Night and day the family members wept and cried out for help. No one went to their rescue. Everyone was too afraid to venture close. Of course curiosity often bells the cat, and so James like every boy in the neighbourhood, though frightened out of his wits, wanted to see with his own eyes.

One afternoon James, under the pretence that he was off to visit his sick godmother, decided to venture out there to see if there was any truth in the rumour of spirits tormenting the said family. In the doorway stood an elderly woman dressed in virtual threads. The doors and windows were wide open but darkness enveloped the inside of the house. Rocks and boulders were hurled from every side of the house, enough to make its occupants beg for mercy publicly. In spite of what was before him, naiveté blindfolded James. It enhanced his prejudice and so he laughed the whole thing off as a prank. James was convinced that there were people hiding out in the nearby bushes. He was adamant: only malicious persons were capable of such acts. He believed such persons were out to discredit, to terrorize, and to besiege the family for their own ends. Thus James believed the whole tale about spirits was just fabricated. His youthfulness and naiveté both continued to blindfold him. Despite all he had seen and heard, James Laport held onto his preconceived reservations and conclusions. These stories were merely unfounded myths and legends. The older he got, the more tenaciously he held onto his conclusions. In spite of his conclusions, he inherited a deep seated suspicion and fear of strangers, particularly elderly men and women. James never trusted strangers after all this. If they were not close to his family, they were not party to his life and narrative. James kept a distance. Albert fitted this category.

Albert: the Grass Cutter

Albert was a lanky individual. Age must have forced him to lean over like a wilting banana tree. His spinal cord leapt out of his back like a camel's hump. His lips receded deep into his mouth; his chin protruded over his chest like an arrow. Although he was of African descent, his eyes were narrowed like an Oriental's. His looks were always suspicious. Albert was always dressed with the same dirty, sweaty khaki suit and a khaki coloured felt hat. Both his suit and hat were in tatters; they were littered with dark brown blotches that looked like banana stains. Frankly the old hat looked like a bird's nest placed upside down over his head and it reached far down over his eyebrows and ears. His pointed nose, long oversized ears and crisscrossed eyes made him the epitome of a wizard. Albert always carried a sickle in his right hand and a bundle of grass under his left arm. His looks, the sickle and the grass made him even more frightening.

One morning, James' father sent him on an errand to his godmother's home. It was about a twenty minute walk from his home. When he approached his godmother's home, James spotted Albert cutting grass just at the entrance. James was in a quandary. The longer he lingered to make time to allow Albert to leave, the longer Albert lingered as well. At one time Albert stood at attention with his sickle placed around his neck. Then he placed his hands behind his back and looked directly in the direction of James. Shivers ran though James' body. By then, time was against James. He had to return home on time to get ready for school. James quietly turned around and walked back home with a single excuse on his mind; "Daddy *Nennenn* was not at home. The house was closed." Daddy of course had no choice but to believe that *Nennenn* must have left home for her garden earlier than usual.

Later that evening James' father came home with a frown on his face and shouted, "Come here, you little brat! Please tell me exactly what happened this morning. Why was it that you never got to your godmother's home?" Before little James could respond, his father broke into laughter. The laughter made James a little apprehensive and befuddled. One minute his father was dead serious and the next minute he was roaring with laughter. Then his father said, 'It was Mr. Albert, wasn't it?' James shamefacedly admitted, "Yes it was. He was standing in the way and I did not trust him. He looked like a cross between an elf and a wizard." James's father roared even louder. It was then that James understood that Albert had been watching him all along. He knew that Albert was aware James was terrified of him. Of course Albert joined in the fray and played the game. He scared the hell out of poor little James; plus he took equal pleasure in sharing the fun with James' father. Even though James understood Albert exploited his fear of him, such knowledge did very little to quell James' suspicion of Albert and the same for other elderly folks in the neighbourhood and beyond.

The Dentures' Story

Far worse was the day when James was visiting his ailing nanny. An elderly gentleman walked into the house. Then, unannounced, the gentleman grabbed a drinking glass and filled it with water. He pushed his fingers into his upper mouth, grabbed hold of his teeth, gum, palate and all and plunged them into the glass of water. He did the same with the lower range of teeth. The sight of this was just too much drama for James. His mouth dropped open. His little limbs too melted like butter in the sweltering sun. He felt his hips giving way and his knees were like rattles. *His first thought was: I'm dead! This man will eat me!* He did not wait to see whether fangs would grow out of the man's bare gums. James pulled himself together, steadied his trembling knees and sped off home as fast as his feet would run.

He arrived home breathless. He fell into his mother's arms. His poor mother was stunned. She kept asking him for quite a while, 'What is the matter?' She shook him several times. Breathlessly he told her what he had seen. With disbelief in her looks and voice, she said, "Boy that's dentures." "Dentures, what's that?" James asked his mother. "False teeth," his mother explained. James was still not willing to trust anybody who walks into a home, pulls his teeth and gums out of his mouth and put them into a glass of water. No! That was beyond James' imagination. Besides, there had been too many stories of missing children, and he was not prepared to be the meal of demons.

The Lajablès and the Accident

The night was still in its infancy. There was a loud bang. A car ran off the road and rolled down into a precipice. The entire neighbourhood gathered to witness what had happened. People were pressed as closely as possible to look down into the precipice, while some men tried to rescue the driver from the crash. Suddenly a man in the crowd shouted in Creole something like, "A cow foot just step over my foot." The crowd responded in Creole *"an lajablés"*. The reaction of the crowd was instantaneous. Immediately, everyone scattered and then formed themselves into a neat circle. The people searched each other's feet to see who it was. A little old hag meanwhile desperately covered her feet. She hustled her way out of the crowd. In the hustle and bustle she managed to elude the eyes of everyone. The driver escaped unscathed. He was grateful that the community had come to his rescue. After he had thanked the crowd, he told his story. He was driving round the bend, he said, and a tall beautiful woman was standing in the middle of the road. He swerved to the right to avoid hitting her and he went over the precipice. James was not convinced. He still insisted that the stories and events were mere myths and legends.

Chapter Two

Adolescent Years

By the time he had reached his adolescent years, James had dismissed all the myths and legends as nonsense, even though some of these same stories were reinforced again and again by his grandfather from Solfatara Town. His grandpa told many stories of his personal encounters during his years of courtship when he travelled the roads between Solfatara Town and *Mopo* Village at odd hours of the night. Time went by quickly. By the time he was twelve, the priesthood occupied James' mind. Thus he felt obliged to dismiss all myths and legends. James considered it all unnecessary garbage and baggage, and nothing useful for priestly ministry. This attitude was further enforced by his departure to pursue studies overseas and his interaction with highly cultured individuals: persons whose minds were reformed by Western influence, and who behaved as if their new found-culture was superior to that of the people who held on to such myths and legends.

In the triad of Afro-Caribbean and Western cultures such myths and legends were often considered unnecessary encumbrances. Even though myths and legends were the cobbler's last nails to keep his shoe and its sole together for the last leg of a journey, he would have still dismissed them as useless.

James Laport never anticipated that these same old myths and legends would be very much alive as a sub-culture in the churches of Helen Island. God has a strange sense of humour. He has some very unusual ways of preparing every Jonah for each journey to Nineveh. Later James would come to realize the reality of their existence and how they were intertwined in the faith of Catholics and non- Catholics as well. All too soon James realized that what he once reckoned were myths and legends were indeed the high occult sciences of the day. It finally dawned on James Laport that these same myths and legends exist in close proximity to the realm of faith among believers of various religious denominations. Sometimes, those who appear to be the best Christians and philanthropists on the surface, may just be the biggest witches or wizards on the block. All along James was like a Jonah in the making, unknown to him.

Popular Syncretism

James believed that Black Magic and White Magic, ghosts and spirits, were just phantoms of creative imaginations and mischievous minds. He was thoroughly convinced such stories were deliberately invented to intimidate people's minds and to instill fear. James became a priest and was affectionately called Fr. Laport by his parishioners. One day, as a priest, he visited the French Caribbean island of Guadeloupe. Walking through the streets, he stumbled across the local produce market. Curiosity urged him to walk through the market to savour some of the local culture. Just at the entrance, Fr. Laport spotted a well decorated stall with religious icons, rosaries, etcetera on sale. He was quite impressed since he had never seen anything like that in his native country. He drew closer to the stall, only to be stunned by what he saw: '*Rituel de Magie Noire* and *Rituel de Magie Blanche*' on sale, side by side with the religious items and icons. 'What an unholy marriage,' he said to himself, 'between the sacred and the profane!' This was an unusual form of popular syncretism unparalleled by anything he had ever witnessed before. Here was popular religiosity encouraging the sale of *black and white magic* side by side with the well recognized special Catholic items and icons used officially in Catholicism.

The thought permeated his mind for a long while. At that point, his mind flashed back to his childhood days. The stories that had at one time both intrigued and terrified him were now sinking in a little deeper but were even more intriguing. The fact that there were rituals for these crafts meant that they were no longer stories but that they did in fact exist. Still, Fr. Laport never thought that all of this would ever have any bearing on his priestly ministry. He never thought about it that day in the market in connection with his work.

It was on his first assignment in Solfatara Town that Fr. Laport had his first rude awakening when confronted by the spirit world. Solfatara Town was his "Open University". It was there that his early childhood revisited and confronted him in a way which he least expected.

To put it more succinctly, the stories were not myths. The elders were simply handing down the oral traditions that inherently were vestiges of African culture which had survived the onslaughts of slavery and colonialism and endured as a subculture in the Diaspora. Africans in the Diaspora were like leopards. They had not changed their spots. They hid behind western culture to be socially accepted but they were Africans at heart and in spirit.

Sadly, Fr. Laport never realized the family and community soirees were more than just *Listwa* time, more than just storytelling. They were nights of enculturation. However, the dilemma he faced was that, during the enculturation *soirees,* the notion of faith never featured. The role of the priests never featured either and it is likely that is where the disconnection between the vestiges of African traditions and religion may have occurred.

It was therefore much later that Fr. Laport discovered that culture and religion have intricately intertwined and that certain myths and legends have their place in faith. In fact for centuries they have contributed to the birth of both traditions and religions. As a priest in his home country, Fr. Laport would eventually come to the realization that he would have to deal with the same issues which he once frowned upon as mere fairy tales.

Solfatara Town brought him back to reality. His subsequent parishes similarly taught him that such issues, though inconsistent with the principles of faith and Catholicism, were ever present in the Caribbean culture. They were very much part and parcel of popular religion in the Caribbean in the twentieth century and would continue to be so into the twenty-first century. For effective priestly ministry and in an effort to win souls back to the Lord, it was imperative that a priest be familiar with those fragments of African culture that still linger within the people's consciousness and influence their faith and patterns of judgement. Thus, through a faith-filled ministry, he must do all within his power along with God's grace to help win back as many souls as possible to the Lord. It is his duty to help others understand the irreconcilable nature of good and evil.

The talk of cults had never cropped up in his priestly experiences. *Black mass* was mentioned, but not to a great extent. When it was mentioned, little James merely thought it meant that the members of the clergy wore black vestments as they did in those days for the celebration of Masses for the dead and at funerals. It would be later in life that Fr. Laport would come to know the drastic difference which exists between the cultic *black mass* and the official Mass at which black vestments were worn.

Geckoville

Shortly after his ordination to the Deaconate, James Laport, was assigned to the Archangel Parish Church in Geckoville, where he spent one year preparing for his priestly ordination. He knew nothing about Geckoville. When his bishop assigned him there, his immediate question to the bishop was, "What's there?" "There is a parish there and you will be working with the Parish Priest as his assistant during your deaconate." What further explanation did Deacon Laport need at that time? None!

Geckoville had an agriculture-based economy and the people there were wonderful, humble and very amicable and affable. They were Catholic to the core. However, with time the talk of necromancy reared its ugly head; but of course, it was typical of James Laport to dismiss everything and anything of that realm to the zone of myths and legends. Even though he was persistently told by some parishioners that Geckoville always had a reputation of being the convention centre for witches, he was not convinced.

At that time such talk held no significance for the young deacon. He heard it and dismissed it all as a mere waste of breath. In most recent times, a young boy had just vanished while visiting a public park in Geckoville in the broad midday sun. It was then that Fr. Laport remembered the incident of a few young men who every night, after their nightly rendezvous, were repeatedly accosted by an unchained mule which took great pleasure in kicking and farting in their faces. Tired out by the experience, they devised a plot among themselves. They gathered some bamboo stems, sharpened one end, hid them along the way and proceeded to their rendezvous. On returning home that night, they encountered the mule as usual. As the young men stepped forward, the mule began kicking up a storm with its usual antics. The young men retrieved their bamboo stems and jabbed the mule in the butt, severely wounding it. Sadly, though, it turned out that the mule was the grandfather of one of the young men in the group. The old man's name was Dada. His butt was blistered. The old man died shortly thereafter as a result of infections due to lack of medical treatment and his stubborn reluctance to admit the conditions under which he had received his wounds. Was his grandson amused? No! Was he sorry for his grandpa? No! Outside the Archangel Church, after his grandpa's funeral, the young man's parting words to his departed grandpa were, '*Sa ou fé, sa ou wè. Sa ou planté, sa ou kay wékòlté.*' (What you sow is what you reap). His parting words were words without remorse.

At the time of that incident, rumors were rife in Geckoville of the disappearance of an elderly woman whose mutilated, dismembered remains were later discovered under a *zakasya* tree with various body parts missing. It was alleged that it was a ritual murder. Her eyes had been dug out of her head, her tongue severed, her heart harvested as well as her pubic region. Speculation was rife in the community concerning Dubois' flirtation with sorcery and he was a suspect in the matter. During Dada's funeral, Deacon Laport took the opportunity to remind the congregation of the condition in which the body of the missing woman was found. Dubois was in the congregation. He instantaneously developed a persistent cough, voluntary or involuntary, no one could tell. His cough had made it easy to locate him in the congregation. Deacon Laport recognized that Dubois was visibly uncomfortable. His body twitched from side to side as if begging to put an end to the subject of the old lady's demise. Dubois' coughing and twitching was a distraction for the congregation. From his vantage point, Deacon Laport recognized that Dubois looked as if he was in a quandary and he needed a means of escape. Still coughing, Dubois stood up and made his way out of the church. Without a thought, before making his final exit, unaware that he was still within hearing distance, he blurted out: *Sé pa mwen ki pwan fanm-a é tout moun vlé blanmé mwen! "Pa mwen ki pwan tjè'y, pa mwen ki koupé lann'y ébien tiwé zyé'y."* (I'm not the one who abducted the woman! Everyone wants to blame me! I'm not the one who harvested her heart, her tongue and eyes.) Another parishioner, standing near the main entrance where Dubois made his exit replied, *"Lè konsyans an moun lou ou kwè sè kat."* (A conscience under pressure is easily spilled.)

Such exposures made no difference to Deacon Laport's thinking. He was still persistent in his thoughts that all of this was still myths and legends. Would Solfatara Town be the turbulent sea that would awaken his consciousness and bring him home to face the realities of *Listwa Time?*

Chapter Three

Solfatara Town

It was six o'clock in the evening. Dusk and darkness were jostling for space over Solfatara Town. The bells of Assumption Catholic Church were chiming the last melodies of the Angelus. Darkness slowly crept over Solfatara chasing all hustlers off the streets. Assumption was the only hub of activity whenever Nyx sprawled its wings and talons over Solfatara Town. Otherwise, the main streets of Solfatara Town were desolate. In the remote corners and in the back streets, the rum shops attracted their usual clients. The rumbling muffled sound of voices carried by the wind reminded passersby that Solfatara was not a cemetery with paved roads, and streets with lights. Sometimes the rumblings sounded like ghosts' conventions. On the periphery of the town the constant bashing of the waves gave the town its unique melody and air of tranquility, interrupted at daybreak by the clamouring voices of fishermen and the sound of boat engines launching out to sea for the day's catch. Towering over all other structures in Solfatara Town was the indomitable belfry of Assumption Catholic Church, the symbol and bastion of Catholicism in Helen Island; a formidable footprint left behind by French missionaries.

Just a stone's throw away from Assumption, protected behind high walls and grilled gates, Fr. Laport, the Associate Pastor of Assumption, concluded the Angelus, blessed his supper and signed himself with the sign of the cross. Then he sat down at the table and nibbled at his supper. The next item on his agenda for the evening was a choir rehearsal in anticipation of the approaching Sunday.

Fr. Laport was still very much a neophyte to the priesthood. The sacred oil had not yet dried off his hands. As a child, he had spent many of his Christmas and summer vacations on the outskirts of Solfatara Town. He had paid no attention to Solfatara's culture and its traditions then. Perhaps all that lingered with him until his priestly assignment there were the nostalgic memories of the sumptuous traditional Kwéyòl cuisine: the tender blue dasheen swamped in local dark brown stewed chicken, fresh vegetable salad draped in homemade vinaigrette, Christophine au gratin, pigeon peas and the roasted sweet potatoes or roasted breadfruit slightly drizzled with vinaigrette, often served with a hot cup of undiluted milk straight from the cow. Wow! Bread was a delicacy in the countryside in those days. Breakfast consisted of roasted breadfruit and hot cow's milk, the taste of which has never been the same in Félicitéville.

By seven o'clock in the evening voices emerged from all directions adjacent to the presbytery. The youth choir members were trying to lure Fr. Laport from his supper to the church on time. Fr. Laport did not know that this night in question was his night of initiation, his night of baptism by fire.

Midway during the choir rehearsal, a woman carrying her infant in her arms, accompanied by two other women, approached Fr. Laport and asked to have a word with him. Excusing himself, he turned to the woman "Fadda, my little daughter is seeing spirits." At the sound of the word 'spirit' his heart sank to his feet. Fr. Laport, oblivious of his surroundings shouted: "What? Spirits!" He threw his arms up into the heavens and said to the women, "Sit here and wait a while."

His heels hardly touched the ground as he made his exit from the church back to the presbytery. His mind was like a cauldron burning with questions. His heart was wrapped in flames. His knees were knocking. They had to bear their fair share carrying him back to the presbytery. Instantly, he recalled that the seminary had never trained him for such pastoral encounters and more so, the Pastor, Fr. Fallon, was out of reach. Fr. Laport's world was collapsing around him. When he arrived at the presbytery, he slammed himself into a chair. For well over thirty minutes, he ranted and raved with God for having landed him into such a predicament like this, unprepared. He protested over and over again, 'God, I'm not prepared for this. I was not trained in handling exorcisms!' It seemed like the more he ranted and raved and protested, the more God was having a field day with him. At one point Fr. Laport felt like one of the prophets of Baal "The gods," he cried, 'they have a sense of humour that's not amusing in the time of crisis!' Again he cried out, "I'm not a prophet of Baal, you know! Like Elijah, I'm your servant, O God. Tell me what to do."

Suddenly Fr. Laport fell silent, worn out by his own excitement. Silently a voice said to him, 'Father, pick up the telephone, call and ask some elderly members of the parish prayer group to join you in prayer before the Blessed Sacrament and go back to Assumption. I will guide you through it all.'

A bulwark of faith, affectionately nicknamed Mama Marianna by Fr. Laport himself, came to mind. Fr. Laport dialed her number and on the first ring, her stately voice was heard on the other end of the line:

"Hello!"

"Yes Mama Marianna."

"Yes, Fr. Laport, good evening and how can I help you?"

"The Lord has placed me in an unusual predicament. He has sent me my first challenge of faith."

"Now, tell me Father, what is it?"

Fr. Laport briefed Mama Marianna who readily agreed to call in her prayer squad to assist with prayers before the Blessed Sacrament.

The Tip of the Iceberg

Still very much unnerved by the incident, Fr. Laport returned to Assumption where the group of ladies and the infant waited patiently. He ushered them into the sacristy and requested two or three members

19

of the choir to assist with prayers. Addressing the infant, the priest asked: "Show me your mummy." The infant identified her correctly and likewise with every other person in the room. The infant was persistent in pointing in the direction of the spirit and identified it as a man. Fr. Laport started off by invoking the name of Jesus and commanding the spirit to come to Jesus and be submissive to the command of Jesus. The session must have lasted for almost an hour when finally a cross was placed over the infant's face; she kissed the cross, coughed a little and immediately fell asleep.

Fr. Laport was relieved. The drama was over. The situation was under control. At least that was what he thought. Later that night, the infant appeared to him in a dream and said: "Thank you for freeing me from the spirit of Bolo." Talk about a rude awakening to the world of spirits. Early the next morning, Fr. Laport summoned the infant's mother to see him and asked: 'Who is Bolo?' The flabbergasted mother stood silent for a while. Then she blurted out, 'That's an old man, a neighbour of mine. He died a few months ago. Fadda he was a very wicked man.' Fr. Laport then shared his dream with the infant's mother, after which they each went their separate ways. No doubt Fr. Laport was convinced that the drama with spirits and the dead was now behind him. At least that was what he thought. But it was just the tip of the iceberg.

Father Fallon's Prediction

The next morning Fr. Fallon and Fr. Laport, after the morning's Mass, stood under the veranda of the presbytery, directly under the shadow of a statue of the Blessed Virgin Mary. They were reminiscing over the events of the previous day. Fr. Fallon commented: "This is an ideal venue for doing exorcisms." Gosh! It was like prophecy come true. The words were hardly out of his mouth when an embattled elderly woman walked through the gates and showered the priests with her woes. She was convinced that she was possessed by some evil spirits. Moreover, she was convinced that her neighbour, a highly respected Masonic aristocrat from Félicitéville, was responsible for her woes. Luckily, on the day in question, an exorcist from the United States was visiting Solfatara Town.

The visiting priest willingly assisted Fr. Fallon and Fr. Laport. He taught them both the principles of the exorcism while he himself undertook the first phase of exorcism. At the end of the morning's session the woman looked young. She was beautiful again but the exorcist warned Frs. Fallon and Laport "You still have a great deal of work to do with her." At the sound of his words, some novices, who had assisted with the prayer ministry during the exorcism, grew red in the face. Their expression betrayed their thoughts: *'Take this thing somewhere else.'* They were like scared rats behind the convent walls. One of the young postulants, Sister Pat, covered her ears while Sister Wisdom wrapped her clothes tightly around her as if they were her only protective armory. Sisters Paul Claude and Jacintha stood rigid with shrugged shoulders looking like mountains ready to crumble into molehills. Mother Superior was still clutching her rosary, while Fr. Laport looked dazed. The collective, unspoken consensus was, *'Do we have to go through this again?'* The answer was, 'Yes!' The question was not *'when?'* but *'how soon?'*

Early next morning the woman attended Holy Mass and requested confession. Still very apprehensive, Fr. Laport decided to hear her confession at the altar rail within sight of those who lingered after the morning Mass for their private devotion; they would be nearby in the event of any manifestations. Sitting on a chair just a stone's throw away from the Blessed Sacrament, the priest asked the penitent to kneel. As she knelt, her knees hit the floor of the church. The church shook as if tectonic plates were shifting, loud enough to attract the attention of all in the church. Judging by the people's reaction, everyone thought that it was an earthquake, but the bang was too instantaneous and short-lived to be an earthquake. Shaken to their wits, the people then left one by one and stood outside looking in, as if to protect the priest from a distance in the event of a second tremor.

From what Fr. Laport had gathered, the church was the woman's last resort in her search for deliverance. The witchdoctors had had a "field day" with her purse. However, no matter how many eggs she had rubbed under her arms and had thrown backward into the sea, there was no letting up of the spirits' stronghold on her life. Instead, things got worse steadily. When she was nearly broke, she decided to seek help from the church.

After confession, she kissed Fr. Laport goodbye on his cheek. Her lips were as cold as frozen meat. "Gosh!" he thought. "Is this a virtual encounter with the devil itself or what? Or was the water receding? Was the iceberg growing out of the water that quickly?" These were just rhetorical questions, but it was something he had to figure out for himself as a neophyte priest and exorcist.

The prediction of the visiting exorcist was true. Her initial transformation was only a mask of deception. Her exorcism demanded much more than one session. After five long working sessions with her, Fr. Laport realized that the waves were far from receding. The journey certainly looked much longer than was initially anticipated. Fr. Laport realised that her deliverance demanded prayer, fasting and sacrifice. By then it was clear to Fr. Laport that her deliverance could not be achieved in mere hours, days, weeks, or even months. In spite of all his human and priestly efforts, he had to wait in faith for the Lord to act. Discernment, wisdom and faith are gifts from the Lord and are always crucial to success. These gifts are given to people in small measures and Fr. Laport was prepared to wait for the Lord to act when the time was right. They are the true maps to guide Fr. Laport to the root of the problem. For well over three months, Fr. Laport and his team had spent many nights and days before the Blessed Sacrament in prayer. It was there that the Holy Spirit revealed to him that this woman was inflicted with the spirit of her deceased brother who had died by drowning and whose body had never been recovered. There had never been a funeral or a memorial Mass offered in his memory. His soul seemed restless.

One day, while Fr. Laport was at prayer, a horrible looking person emerged from what looked like a turbulent sea. He claimed that he was the brother of the possessed woman. After he was repeatedly asked his name, he revealed his true identity and once more quickly disappeared into the sea. Shortly thereafter, Fr. Laport sent for the possessed woman and divulged the name to her. She immediately admitted, "That was my brother. He died by drowning and we never recovered his body." This revelation was the first step in the right direction. Three times the soul of her brother was called by name and commanded to go to Jesus that Jesus may tell him what to do. After this invocation, his soul was commended to the Lord so that it would rest in peace like the souls of all the faithful departed. Subsequent to this short rite, three requiem Masses (Masses celebrated in memory of the dead, asking God to grant eternal rest to the deceased) were celebrated in his memory. The woman was completely delivered at the end of this long journey which lasted for well over three months.

By this time, news of the two events had spread like wild-fire through the length and breadth of Solfatara Town and beyond. All of Helen Island was on edge and ready to make pilgrimages to Solfatara Town, bringing with them all the afflicted. It was like bees converging on a honey pot and everyone was running towards it rather than running away from it. Meanwhile, Fr. Laport felt as if his feet had sunk into the deep when he least expected it. The burning question for him was: "When will this nightmare end so that I can assume my conventional parochial duties?" No answer was forthcoming. Instead the cases kept coming fast and furiously.

Jovana's Ordeal

It was a hectic weekend. A youth retreat was in its final hours. It was Sunday afternoon about four o'clock. Parents, well-wishers and others gathered in an adjacent school near Assumption along with the youths on retreat for the closing Mass. All items on the agenda seemed to fall into place without a hitch. Everyone was in very high spirits. Just at the Post Communion Prayer, the solemnity of the event was rudely interrupted when a voice was heard, 'Jovana, watch out!' Almost instantaneously, Jovana received a slap right across her face, loud enough for everyone in the congregation to hear. But no one in the congregation saw from where the slap emanated. Only Harricia, the young lady who alerted Jovana, witnessed the entire episode. Harricia fainted at the sound of the slap. Upon recovery, Harricia recounted that she had seen Jovana's grandfather, Gerald, invoking the spirit of Jovana's deceased father, John, at her father's tomb. However, John's spirit was so irate that he turned on Jovana and slapped her, rather than his own father. When the story reached the ears of the people in Solfatara Town, it was alleged that Jovana, being the eldest child of her deceased father, was destined to be sacrificed in order that Gerald would inherit his son's estate.

At a subsequent prayer session, Jovana had a similar experience. While at prayer with the rest of the youths, she suddenly received another slap, loud enough to be heard by all present. At that instant she fainted, causing panic among the gathering. The sequence of events and manifestations, starting with the baby who saw the spirit of Bolo, the possessed woman and Jovana's second experience, was by now unnerving for Fr. Laport who was a newly ordained priest. What made matters even more unnerving for him was that the Pastor, Fr. Fallon had made a quick exit on his way to an adjacent parish, leaving his Associate Pastor to paddle the canoe in what Fr. Laport termed: *In Turbulent Waters.*

The youths, although in a state of agitation, settled down quickly. Fr. Laport immediately divided the group into two sections: one group was commissioned to go before the Blessed Sacrament and do nothing else but recite the Holy Rosary unceasingly. That night non-believers in the rosary were converted. They became apostles of the rosary for other youths. It was not a secondhand experience narrated to them. No! Each one in his or her own way had a personal experience of the power of Mary as intercessor in heaven.

The other young people accompanied Fr. Laport in praying over Jovana until she recovered fully. Upon recovery, her story was identical to that which was recounted earlier. Nothing remained concealed in Solfatara Town. Even if the event took place behind sealed walls and locked doors, the grapevine would have it in seconds. By the time the prayer meeting had ended, news of Jovana's second episode was already in circulation. Meanwhile it was reported, according to the rumor mill, that her grandfather, Gerald, was seen leaving Ma Fano's house at the time of the incident. Rumor had it then that Ma Fano was a witch. Fr. Laport could not fathom the connection between the two incidents. Fr. Laport was convinced that God would reveal them in good time.

These manifestations were just too many in a short space of time and Fr. Laport was already showing signs of fatigue. The only two-line mantra he had made his own was: "Lord let this go away! Let it be the iceberg itself!" At least he wished it was, but only time would tell.

Lenten Outreach

The Lenten season was quickly approaching. Plans were afoot for a massive evangelization outreach program. For the first three weeks of Lent, all hands were on deck: the music ministry was fired up, ushers, prayer teams, stage management team and preachers for the respective nights all made preparations. All parishioners in Solfatara Town too were on fire. Expectation was at fever pitch. Everyone who was able to make it came; either on foot, by bus, by car or otherwise. Jones Diddy came riding on his donkey. All gathered in the town's playing field for three consecutive weeks to listen to the Word of God and to turn as many hearts back to the Lord as possible. The outreach program was a novelty for Assumption. It did create its intended impact as Frs. Fallon and Laport had hoped. People returned to church in droves.

The liturgies were living testimonies of hearts won over by the Lord. More and more accommodation was needed to make everyone feel at home but the people never minded being crowded. They endured standing throughout the long liturgies.

In the hour of glory, why ponder over adversity? Fr. Fallon, in his wisdom, had repeatedly warned members of the evangelization team, "Where the Lord is building a chapel, Satan is building a cathedral." His words fell on deaf ears. In the euphoria of the moment, everyone was caught up in the excitement of the experience and its impact on lukewarm Catholics. Indeed, as in the days of Job, Satan was seated in the congregation seeking those he could seduce into his convoy of demons.

A Demon in the Crowd

Little did Frs. Fallon and Laport and the planners anticipate the unsealing of a Pandora's Box; and the events that were to follow were like the floodgates left opened at the high point of the hurricane season. It was seven o'clock Sunday evening. After Praise and Worship and the exposition of the Blessed Sacrament, the faithful gathered outside of Assumption, waiting to process to the town's playing field. On approaching the gathering, Fr. Laport caught sight of something unusual. At first glance, it looked like a pig standing tall on its hind legs. Fr. Laport turned to an altar server who followed him and asked, "What's a pig doing in the gathering?" The altar server's eyes narrowed and ruts grew out of his forehead. At first he was speechless. He replied with his index finger over his lips, "No Father, it's not a pig. It has a human body."

"Oh gosh! Not again!" The words were hardly on his lips, but his blood was already running cold. "No, not another encounter," he said under his breath, trying to conceal any trace of fear which could betray his lack of faith in the presence of the faithful.

As he drew closer to the gathering, Fr. Laport sprinkled the people with holy water. The possessed individual made a desperate dash to get away, out of the reach of the holy water. It was at this point that people in the crowd recognized her presence and a woman in the crowd shouted, *"Mi an kochon moun anpami nou wi."* Another responded, "It's not a human pig. It's a demon, the devil himself." At that point the individual grunted like a real pig. Some persons in the crowd, recognizing the individual, pleaded with Fr. Laport to take her into the church and pray over her. Instead of proceeding to the intended venue that night, the crowd opted to return to the church and spend the night in prayer before the Blessed Sacrament, while a group of devotees assisted Fr. Laport with the rite of exorcism. O what a night of hell on earth! A night confronted by things both visible and invisible! Things never heard of before! Fr. Laport had seen the movie, *The Exorcist* in his early days as a seminarian, but he never expected to have to perform any exorcisms as a priest in the twentieth century. No! At least not in his homeland, despite all the *Anansi* stories he had listened to in his childhood.

He believed Helen Island was still ninety-eight percent Catholic. In other words, Helen was at the time ninety-eight percent Christian. Christians, he was convinced, had renounced the devil and his works and promises and had given themselves to the Lord through the hands of the Blessed Virgin Mary. However Fr. Laport would sooner than later discover that this presumption was wrong. Catholicism for some was a charade. It was a religion of convenience and social acceptability. The Creed was poetry recited; not really accepted as the *Credo* of the children of God baptized into Christ Jesus. The shortest way up the social ladder was conformity. There was no adherence to the doctrine proffered by the apostles. It was recited by many Catholics like parrots. The faith of some Catholics was based on material gain rather than the submission of will to God.

Time and time again, during the exorcism, the individual confronted and challenged Fr. Laport, who occasionally resorted to administering some very heavy slaps to the pig-like face. After each slap, the individual's face bled. Each time, she immediately retreated into a corner in the sacristy, adopted a fetal-like position and behaved like a wimp sometimes, or a wounded child longing for attention. Everyone knew this behaviour was a gimmick that had to be dismissed without empathy. Time and time again, the church erupted in loud prayer and praises as if they were in sync with events as they unfolded in the sacristy. It was almost a two-hour battle which seemed like a never ending two-years, when suddenly the spirit complied with the demands of the exorcism and decided to depart. In leaving, it berated the Blessed Virgin Mary, Fr. Laport and his team with the foulest language and threats to their lives.

Amazingly, at the end of the session, there sat, before everyone, a most beautiful young woman, with no fingerprints, no bleeding wounds to the face and with no recollection of what had transpired in the sacristy. That night when the young woman was presented to the congregation, the entire church erupted in a jubilant chorus of praise and thanksgiving. The night ended with Benediction of the Blessed Sacrament. The rest of that week went without a hitch until the Friday night when hell broke loose again.

The Way of the Cross

It was Friday night - a night exclusively reserved for the "Way of the Cross" during the Lenten observances. On the night in question, it was decided that in keeping with the evangelization outreach program, the Way of the Cross would be conducted through the streets of Solfatara Town. The night began on a vibrant note. Large crowds followed and the people's participation was more than anticipated because of the novelty of the experience. Somewhere along the way, in one of the back streets, two notorious Magdalenes of the town started to chastise Fr. Laport, "*Nou pa sav ki sa ki wivé ti nèg sa la, monsenyè-a voyé'y pwéché an légliz-a, i toupatou an lawi-a ka fè dézòd.*" (We do not know what the problem is with this little black boy. He was sent here by the bishop to preach in the church but he is everywhere in the streets kicking up a storm).

Just at that point, the crowds stopped before a very quaint little green house which emitted a very eerie feeling. Presumably, it seemed, Fr. Laport had not had enough challenges on his plate as yet. He unilaterally decided to go in and bless the house. What he encountered was way beyond his imagination and expectation. It was beyond the imagination of his congregation too. All he and his followers knew for certain was this: that night was the genesis of the conversion experience of the two Magdalenes who moments earlier were chastising Fr. Laport. At the end of the drama at the house and the return to the church, the two Magdalenes each went back to their respective homes, picked up a chair each, carried it into the church, placed it just outside of the sanctuary and boldly proclaimed: "From this night onward this will be our place in the church!" What had really happened?

Just as Fr. Laport was making his way into Ma Fano's house, he stumbled but he was supported by two choir members, Harricia and Bellarosa who followed closely behind him. Bellarosa stayed outside weeping because she had seen two hands struggling with Fr. Laport. They attempted to throw him over the steps. Fr. Laport never saw any of this. All he felt was a force pushing him to the ground but the efforts was unsuccessful. Harricia and Bellarosa kept him on his feet and helped him into Ma Fano's house. Every light in the house was switched on, yet an unusual darkness hovered over every space in it. In the center of the sitting room, to his immediate left, was a black dog. It stood there as if it were a fossil frozen from antiquity - its jaw ajar, ready to snarl. Not a sound was heard. It was well poised for an attack but something invisible had restrained it. It neither barked nor moved, nor winked - yet the dog was a living dog.

On his immediate right stood a table covered with bread crumbs and an assortment of lighted coloured candles placed in a circle in the middle of the table. A thick layer of smoke hovered over the candles. The darkness and the smoke filled the rooms with an eerie feeling, but Fr. Laport was still a stranger to the spirit world and did not pay attention to these things. However, when Fr. Laport raised his hand and sprinkled the house and its occupants, Harricia, who had followed him into the house, crumbled to the floor speechless, the pupils of her eyes having receded into her forehead. Some people from the crowd hurriedly grabbed her, carried her out and took her back to the church. Meanwhile there was a loud commotion outside. Some people were kneeling on the rocky street, others holding their heads, others covered their eyes and started calling upon God, *Mon Dyé! Papa Bondyé!* Among those kneeling on the bare gravel were the Magdalenes. They were making public confessions. Cut to the heart, they proclaimed boldly, with no reservation: "There is God and we will follow Him!"

On returning to the church, Harricia was still dazed. Her eyes were transfixed. She appeared as if she were in a different world. She was left in the care of some prayer warriors in the sacristy while Fr. Laport attended to the needs of the wider congregation. He debriefed them as to what exactly had transpired at the scene. One of the Magdalenes came forward and told the whole story. She confessed that she had seen many dead persons whom she recognized running out of Ma Fano's house. Someone or something came running out of every room; every pot and pan that was opened or uncovered that night. Many persons recognized their dead relatives whose souls they had believed were at rest. Fr. Laport, before he departed from Ma Fano's house, invited her to Church on Sunday. She graciously accepted the invitation.

Just then, the events and story surrounding Grandpa Gerald and Ma Fano were recalled to the mind of Fr. Laport. Shortly after Jovana's second episode, Fr. Laport remembered blessing with salt a small white basin left on the presbytery wall just opposite Ma Fano's quaint little green house. He remembered the afternoon when Ma Fano had tried to retrieve the little white basin and how she wept and mourned bitterly. Ma Fano openly confessed that someone was out to do her harm. She complained that the basin was much too heavy, and yet a one-year-old child could have carried this small basin with utmost ease but not Ma Fano on the afternoon in question. She kicked, she tugged, she pulled and dragged at the basin. All her neighbours asked, "What's with you and the basin?" "Nothing!" was her quick response, as if she was annoyed with the entire neighbourhood. In fact, she had openly rebuked them and candidly told them that they were too inquisitive trying to pry into her private business. Her rebuke went a long way to heighten the suspicions the neighbours already had, based on her secluded lifestyle and the unusual characters that frequented her home. Before she was able to take the basin into her house, she had hosed it down. She also did the same to the road.

Harricia's Deliverance

It was late that night when the congregation was dismissed. Many testimonies were given and all that was said corroborated with the Magdalenes' story. Late as it was, Harricia needed urgent attention. By that time, Fr. Fallon, who was attending to an outstation, had returned home. Of course there was a communication mode in Helen Island and more so in Solfatara Town, more efficient than the telephone and television network. It was called "Tell-A-Person". This mode of communication had already transmitted the story. Fr. Fallon met Fr. Laport at the gate of the Presbytery and enquired of him what exactly had transpired.

Fr. Laport hardly had time to open his mouth before the group of young persons who had accompanied him to the gates was divulging information *ad lib*. With the barrage of information thrown at Fr. Fallon, he turned his attention to Fr. Laport once again and asked, "Dear Father, may I ask you where did you send those spirits and souls?" Fr. Laport was speechless for a moment. When he regained his voice, with a quizzical look on his face, and shaking his head, he replied, "Nowhere. Was I supposed to send them somewhere?" "Nowhere," repeated Fr. Fallon. His head danced like Santa Claus. By then Fr. Laport's mind was on fire. He wondered what could be done at this stage. Fr. Fallon retorted, "I think we'll pray over Harricia first and then we'll spend the rest of the night in prayer before the Blessed Sacrament." Without a second thought everyone agreed.

The team gathered in a small makeshift chapel at the Presbytery for the night. They prayed relentlessly for Harricia through the night. During the prayer of exorcism, Harricia coughed violently and persistently. She fell into a deep sleep and then woke up still looking exhausted as if she had walked the length and breadth of Helen Island. Waking out of her daze, she asked "'What's going on? What am I doing here?" After a brief explanation, she remembered being at Ma

Fano's house and that was the last thing that she remembered. Harricia joined the all-night vigil. She had always been a person of tremendous faith and with great zeal for the church. The all-night vigil before the Blessed Sacrament went well. Everyone sat on the bare floor. At times, the group erupted in spontaneous prayers; at other times, they sang spontaneously; and at other times, all maintained a period of total silence until it was rudely interrupted by something unusual.

Somewhere in the wee hours of the morning, exhaustion came upon them. As the hours ticked away, eyes grew heavier and heavier. The chapel gradually became a dormitory. At that crucial moment, something unusual happened. People in the chapel brushed their faces one after another, almost as if it were a ritual. As each person did so, his or her eyes narrowed and heads turned from left to right. Each person looked around as if searching for something or for someone else but no one uttered a word. Fr. Laport, who seemed half asleep, was seen performing the same acts as those who preceded him in the circle. His eyes sprang open; he slapped his mouth as if chasing some fly or an invisible bug; then he jumped to his feet. If there were any visitors outside of the immediate team in the chapel, they would no doubt be left with the distinct impression that it was a well-rehearsed presentation of an unknown ritual. The truth be told, it was not.

The atmosphere in the chapel was frigid and morbid, too eerie to put into words. Something strange was happening. What was it? There was an invisible presence moving around the chapel. It blew like a gentle and soothing wind directly into the mouth of each person. Wow! Wow! People got hysterical. Almost like a chain reaction, a chorus of praises and thanksgiving filled the room. Spontaneously, the names of the Holy Spirit and Holy Michael the Archangel were on the lips of everyone. Before long the atmosphere in the chapel was warm again. Then each person, in turn, told his or her personal experience. The experiences were all identical.

It was then that Fr. Fallon prayed for the souls and commended them to the care of the Lord. He then proceeded to warn the entire group that in future, under such conditions, they should remember to call upon the souls if they are known by name and to command them to go to the Lord and the Lord would tell them what to do. By then Fr. Laport had made himself a silent oath; never again to attempt anything like that!

However, God's ways are beyond our human understanding. Once He has laid His hands upon you, you can wiggle but you can't run and you can't hide. God will find you. It is frightening, yet it is believable. Once your hand has been set to the plough, God will not let you off the plot of land he wants you to sow and to cultivate. God is not a slave master. In a spirit of gentle mastery he will pursue you to the end. He will supply you with all the strength and skills you need to get his task accomplished.

Ma Fano's Confession

There was never a dull day or night in Solfatara Town. On Sunday morning, Ma Fano made her grand entry at Mass. The entire congregation was seized with consternation. Had a pin dropped in the church, its echo would have disturbed the residences as far away as Félicitéville. Every person at Mass that Sunday morning waited with bated breath to see what Ma Fano's next move would be. Certainly the congregation did not give her a prodigal daughter's welcome.

After the Post Communion Prayer, Fr. Laport invited Ma Fano to the lectern to tell her own story. She wanted the people of Solfatara Town to know what had transpired at her quaint little house that night in question. As she made her way to the lectern, Grandpa Gerald's body twitched from side to side, almost like steel forcefully mangled. His face was masked with trepidation. His eccrine glands had conspired to expose his trepidations. It was as if a secret pact has been signed between him and Ma Fano. While his body did all within its power to betray him, a hardly audible murmur of the congregation added even more fuel to the flames. His body and the congregation's undertone spoke one and the same language. Everyone believed there was some form of conspiracy between him and Ma Fano. His reaction begged the question: "Why? Why was this man so visibly nervous and restless?" That was the silent rhetorical question visible on everybody's face. Anyone who was gifted in lip reading would detect the other rhetorical question, mumbled beneath everybody's breath. They asked one to another, "Were they partners in crime?" Speculation and suspicion were rife. Only Ma Fano and Grandpa Gerald knew what each other knew, but thank God Ma Fano's public confession did not take the pin off the grenade. For a moment, the spotlight stayed on Grandpa Gerald until Ma Fano opened her mouth and then all eyes turned in her direction.

Ma Fano limited her confession to her own personal journey. She openly admitted that Fr. Laport had caught her right in the act. Satan was about to make his grand entry when Fr. Laport's presence interrupted him. Satan was really mad. First Satan tried to throw Father off his feet but when he failed, he took his full revenge on Harricia who had followed behind him. He slapped her and threw her to the ground. He wanted her dead so that Father would regret his actions. The Church cried: "Hun! Hun!" Then a deafening silence ensued. Openly, Ma Fano confessed that she'd been a witch for many years. During that time she had disrupted the lives of many people by inflicting pain and distress into their lives. Many people from Solfatara Town and beyond, she admitted, had consulted her to invoke the spirit of the dead for various purposes. She stopped short of naming or implicating anyone by name. All parishioners sat in total disbelief with hands placed firmly on their mouths. Eyes were glued to Ma Fano. Not a syllable fell to the ground as she told her story. In the end she said, "I am prepared to renounce everything and give myself to the Lord. I know it will not be easy. Satan has promised to kill me but you, the people of Solfatara Town, whom I have wounded, please forgive me. Please forgive me I beg you." At that point the congregation squirmed in their seats. Their sighs of relief sounded like an avalanche. Grandpa Gerald was just livid. He was the last to breathe a sigh of relief. It carried the sound of a huge rock plunging into the ocean and its ripples went much further than he himself had ever anticipated. Grandpa's sigh spoke more than words could tell.

Was it a miscalculation on Grandpa Gerald's part? Was his sigh willfully delayed? Was he so lost in his self-created dilemma that he was completely out of sync with the whole congregation?

The black cat was out of the bag. Grandpa Gerald's anger was now directed at Fr. Laport. Despite his nervousness, his eyes shifted from the direction of Ma Fano to the direction of the celebrant's chair where Fr. Laport was sitting. His eyes narrowed. Ruts grew out of his forehead like well-defined furrows ready for cultivation. His shoulders shrugged up to his neck, his lips tightened. His eyes were like flaming arrows with which he tried desperately to pin Fr. Laport to the wall. Fr. Laport was never intimidated by Grandpa's demeanor. Instead, he sprang to his feet and congratulated Ma Fano for taking such a noble and courageous step, and wished her well on her new journey towards a total conversion. He pleaded with the congregation to do the same although he knew well enough that it was indeed a tall order. In Solfatara Town, rumour mills never ceased operation.

The naïve Fr. Laport was now certain that, with the conversion of Ma Fano, and Grandpa Gerald definitely under the watchful eyes of all Solfataraians, the iceberg had melted and the sea was now an open maritime route for safe travel. Fr. Laport was under the misguided belief that his water baptism had seen its day – his initiation rite was complete. He dismissed all fears of drowning in the turbulent waters. The drama had ended. Thanks be to God! The sailors had left the staggering ship. Let them rest in peace! The passengers returned to their respective homes also in peace. But guess what?

The battle had only just started. Ma Fano's life by then had become a living hell. Satan tormented her to her death. The unforgiving public did not make it easy for her. Her victims, while they kept their distance out of fear, contributed much to her demise. Satan had become her archrival. He severely manhandled her. What age did not achieve, and ill health did not hasten, torments, shame and unforgiveness contributed to Ma Fano's earthly demise shortly thereafter. As for Grandpa Gerald, he lived and died in isolation, in an attempt to avoid public humiliation. Despite the passing of both Ma Fano and Grandpa Gerald, the turbulent waters continued to wage on many fronts.

The Battle

In the silence of his room, Fr. Laport sank into his easy chair. Almost instantly his mind started to rummage through the sequence of events as they had unfolded since his arrival in Solfatara Town. 'It was indeed real drama,' he admitted to himself. But it was a drama that his mind could not fathom. He just could not rationalize why such drama had to unfold or coincide with his deployment to Solfatara Town. Nevertheless his questions were all rhetorical. After an undefined period of time brainstorming in search of answers, Fr. Laport gave up and retired into bed. Like Pope Saint John XXIII, he said, "Lord it's your Church. Take care of it. I am going to sleep." But what Fr. Laport did not remember that night was that Prophet Jonah had tried the same gimmick. He ended up in the stomach of a whale and still found himself on the shores of Nineveh where he was sent to call the Ninevites to conversion. Willy-nilly, Jonah had to confront the sins of Nineveh and to bring the people there to conversion. Fr. Laport was neither John XXIII nor Jonah; he considered himself just a simple priest. Was Father Laport looking at his priestly vocation and pastoral ministry through the eyes of God? Was there still more drama to come? Or was Fr. Laport looking as his own priesthood through blinkers? Maybe, just maybe, his experience with Jablé might help remove his blinkers.

Jablé

It was as if Fr. Laport's mind had not yet been sufficiently traumatized by the previous chain of events. One night, while driving from Félicitéville back to Solfatara Town, a lone individual in the remotest and darkest location flagged Fr. Laport to stop. The individual was someone he knew personally; at least he thought he knew him well. However, the young priest chose to err on the side of caution. Instead of the brake, he slammed his foot on the accelerator. Just as he entered Solfatara Town, he spotted the same individual. He pulled up on the side of the street. He called the young man by name and asked, "What were you doing at Tablot?" The question sounded ridiculous to the ears of the young man. "Me," he said while striking his breast, "Not me Father. I was never at Tablot; I've not left the town for the day." For fear of giving further offence to the young man, Fr. Laport said no more and they both treated it as a joke. Then the young man added, pointing his index finger in the direction of Fr. Laport, "Father," he paused. "hope it was not a *Lajablès* or a *Jan gajé* that was trying to block you on the way." They both broke into a heavy roar of laughter and went their separate ways.

Fr. Laport pulled up into his garage and began making his way into the Presbytery to join Fr. Fallon for supper. Just as he was climbing the stairs, there was an uproar in the cellar, loud enough to attract the attention of Fr. Fallon and draw him away from the dinner table to enquire what was happening. Fr. Laport was just as alarmed as Fr. Fallon. Fr. Fallon immediately went to his office and returned with a vial of blessed salt. Together, Fr. Fallon and Fr. Laport went around and blessed the cellar and the presbytery. During the blessing an unusually large cat scampered across the yard and disappeared into the parish hall.

Throughout the night both of the priests were kept awake by the mournful cry of a dying person. Out of deep concern, the priests searched the yard and cellar but came up empty handed. Two days later a young man arrived with news that there was a strange sight and stench on the stage in the parish hall that warranted the attention of the both Frs. Fallon and Laport.

Unbelievable, yet true, the sight was a dead creature: the upper half of the creature was that of a white and ginger coloured cat and the lower extremities of a human person. "My God, what is this?" Fr. Fallon shouted. Almost oblivious to his surroundings, Fr. Laport asked out aloud, "What on earth am I doing in this God-forsaken place?" He added quickly, "Sorry it was the slip of an unguarded tongue speaking under extreme pressure." Yet, Fr. Laport knew deep within his heart that he would not drown. He knew that God was there with him. God was his anchor in the midst of the turbulent waters.

There was much ado over the atrocity lying there before them. A group of spectators had gathered. The next question was 'How were they to dispose of the remains?' The police were notified and the all clear was given for the remains to be disposed of as the Pastor, Fr. Fallon, thought best. The poor old parish gardener, Mr. Knowles, was saddled with the responsibility of loading the remains of the creature unto a wheel barrow and wheeling it away. The poor gardener swore to God he had lifted and wheeled well over a ton of lead. It was so heavy. He went to bury it outside of the parish burial ground. The "Tell-a-person" communication system was fully operational so by this time the grapevine had the whole story.

Before the gardener arrived at the burial site, the whole of Solfatara Town had gathered there. The last missing link in the puzzle was to indentify the individual. With bated breath and heightened curiosity, everyone waited for the news of any missing person. It was long in coming. However, the missing person was not from Solfatara Town, not even from Helen Island but the neighbouring island of Carama. What was Jablé doing all the way in Helen Island and in Solfatara Town? It was everyone's guess. Did Jablé's presence and his untimely demise there in Solfatara Town say something about the nature of Solfatara Town and the dark practices of its dwellers?

It had been said that the living, flesh and bones, were not the only "living inhabitants" in Solfatara Town; that the sacred and profane lived side by side, and that some saints and demons shared a soul. It was a mystery Fr. Laport had tried the best he could to understand. This notion of a person possessing two spirits in one soul or two souls in one body without any conflict of interest had been mind boggling for him. He could not fathom how such a person could be at peace with himself/herself; living in two worlds, yet possessing one body. He often wondered how it was possible to live a life of such deep hypocrisy. The more he prayed and studied the scriptures and the more exorcisms he performed, the harder it was for him to reconcile the differences between the two worlds - the sacred and the profane.

Solfatara Town taught Fr. Laport many such lessons in the most painful way. He learned that people achieved wealth, status, power and glory at the expense of their human souls. It was mind-boggling the things people would do to achieve their own ends. A one-time friend and politician reminded him of this when he said, "Father, when it comes to elections, if one has to sleep with the devil to win, that's what it takes." Nothing would stop a gluttonous person from selling his or her own soul for a desire, not even a need.

In the deliverance of the demoniac, it was not the devils who were asked to leave town. Even when the demoniac terrorized the villagers, he was never asked to leave. When Jesus delivered the demoniac from the claws of two thousand spirits, he was sent packing. He was sent packing for the simple reason that he had destroyed a herd of two thousand pigs to save one individual. He touched the villagers where it pained them the most. He played with their economy. In the name of power, wealth and status the soul of man is often the sacrifice. Who next will have to pay the price before someone learns, before it's too late? Are the *poto légliz* hopeful examples?

Maybe Carmen's life's story might cast some light on this question. Carmen and Grandpa Gerald were *poto légliz*. In Fr. Laport's estimation of them, Grandpa Gerald and Carmen were just two examples. Their dabbling with the occult did not make them hopeful examples. They did not meet the criterion set out for firm believers. According to St. Paul, "The life and death of each of us has its influence on others; if we live, we live for the Lord; if we die, we die for the Lord. So alive or dead we belong to the Lord (Rom.14:7-8)." Fr. Laport believed that the priority of every *poto légliz* is to recognise that he or she is no longer his or her own property. All believers in Christ have been bought and paid for with the currency of Christ's blood (1Pet.1:19).

Carmen and the Frog

It was a weekday. Carmen was noticeably absent from Mass. She was always first on the Communion line. It was six thirty in the morning when Mass concluded. Out of concern, Fr. Laport enquired about her. He was told that she was badly burnt and had been hospitalized from the previous night. His heart was filled with empathy for her. At his earliest convenience that morning, Fr. Laport paid Carmen a visit at the hospital. She was burnt from the back of her head to the back of her knees. Her condition was heart-wrenching. Fr. Laport's face was masked with compassion for her. She was lying prostrate on the bed, draped with a mosquito net over her to keep flies and other contaminants away from her well roasted back.

"Poor Carmen," he said, with his voice trembling, "How did you manage to burn yourself like that?" Sheepishly she glanced at him, quickly removed her eyes from his glance and replied in her typical colloquial way, "Fadda I did not burn myself hun. Ma Oliva that burn me last night *oui*." Carmen's response was like a face wash for Fr. Laport. He cupped his hands. He lifted them to his face and wiped his face over and over again. Within seconds the mask of compassion was replaced by a mask of rage and anger. "What?" Fr. Laport was livid. His voice echoed through the ward. Every patient turned in the direction of Carmen's bed. Recognising that he had created a scene, Fr. Laport lowered his voice and asked, "Why would somebody do this to another person? This is unconscionable!" persisted Fr. Laport. At this point the little old lady went silent. The silence was long and ambiguous. Fr. Laport thought to himself, "Maybe Carmen needed sometime to herself to cope with her pains." He wished her well and walked away.

On his way back to the Presbytery, Fr. Laport found it necessary to have a word with Ma Oliva. He stopped over by her shop and greeted her: "Good morning Ma Oliva! How are you? Do you have breakfast for a starving priest?" "Of course Father, please come right in." Ma Oliva was busy preparing breakfast for Fr. Laport. In his own mind he questioned the tranquility with which Ma Oliva carried herself around the house and in the kitchen. He even questioned the ease with which she conversed with him but maintained his silence, waiting for the opportune moment to pose his question. Fr. Laport was slow but it was good that he was restrained. Otherwise, he may have posed his questions with a certain bias that would have long term negative effects on his pastoral relationship with Ma Oliva. Instead he dilly-dallied with his questions. Harriet, another parishioner, arrived at Ma Oliva's door and pre-empted Fr. Laport's actions. As soon as Ma Oliva opened the door, Harriet bolted in and blurted out, "*Ma Oliva, mwen tan moun ka di toupatou ou bwilé Carmen yé oswè.*"

42

(Mrs. Oliver, there is a rumor around town that you burnt Carmen last night) *"Mwen,"* Ma Oliva interrupted, *"An kwapo ki antwé andidan tjwizin mwen yé oswè èk mwen vide dlo cho asou'y."* (Me! A frog intruded into my kitchen last night and I poured boiling water over it).

The conversation took on new meaning immediately. "Carmen! Carmen!" Ma Oliva waved her right index finger in Harriet's face, almost like a conductor, conducting an orchestra, "Carmen did you say?" asked Ma Oliva with the most incredulous look on her face, hoping that Harriet had mistaken her identities and that Carmen and Ma Oliva were not the parties involved in this drama. To ascertain that she, Ma Oliva, was not involved and that Harriet was wrong in her accusations, Ma Oliva interjected, "But Carmen is in church morning, noon and night." Harriet interrupted Ma Oliva, "Yes Mistress," she stressed, "but de priest dem never see her take de communion out of her mouth when she kneel down and pretend is pray she praying. She always have her handkerchief in her hand when she going for communion." Ma Oliva's eyes focused hard on Harriet's face. Fr. Laport sat rigid, glued to his chair. Not a word emerged from his lips. Silently, he told himself: 'Patience is a virtue.' Harriet had no idea that Fr. Laport was seated at the dining table but once she had delivered the message and got Ma Oliva's side of the story, she was out of the door like a flash. Harriet must have been one of the chief engineers at the rumour mill. Fr. Laport sank deeper and deeper into his seat thinking, "Thank God I did not chastise the poor woman."

Fr. Laport, fearing that he would be embroiled in the matter begged to take his leave. Ma Oliva would not hear of it. She wanted him to know that she was innocent and took no responsibility for the pain and anguish of Carmen. By then anger and rage had fueled Ma Oliva's sentiments towards the whole drama. Her voice, in defense of her reputation, sounded like a gong. No one could restrain her words at that point. Fr. Laport feared that her anger could have led to a stroke or perhaps more fatally, a heart attack. He quickly interjected:

"Heck," he said, "'I'm afraid of frogs myself. If I were in your place, I'd do the same. A frog's place is in the wild." Nevertheless he thought to himself, 'a human life was at stake here. But why would a human being want to transform into a creature? God made humankind in his own image and likeness and has given humankind authority and dominion over all creatures, all the works of his hand. Why should a person then revert to a substandard creature? That's an abomination." With such thoughts spoken in a soothing tone of voice, Fr. Laport was able to tone down Ma Oliva's anger and to prepare her for the barrage of unwanted sympathizers who filed up to her door just to satisfy their own curiosity at the expense of Ma Oliva's distress.

While Fr. Laport consoled Ma Oliva, his mind was running amuck. All the stories his grandfather had narrated to him during his early childhood, while vacationing in Solfatara Town came flooding through his mind. He remembered his grandfather encountering a coffin at the crossroads on his way home one night. The coffin would not allow him to move one step forward or one step backward. His grandfather's only option was to remove his shirt, twist it into a pad and place it on the coffin. Then he lit his pipe and sat on the coffin through the night.

In the wee hours of the morning, whoever the person was, started his pleading: *"Misye-a, souplé mwen ka mandé'w, mew ka plédé épi'w lajé mewn avan sòlèy lévé, souplé misye-a souplé mwen ka mandé'w."* (Sir, please set me free before sunrise. Please sir, I am begging you). However, all his pleas, as hard as he tried, fell on Fr. Laport's grandfather's deaf ears. By sunrise, the individual was left with no option but to reveal his identity and paid the consequences of his action with his life. He committed suicide that same day. The flood gates were opened and a flood of memories gushed through Fr. Laport's mind. Many similar stories which he had not paid heed to in the past, flooded through Fr. Laport's mind now.

Fr. Laport recalled the night when his eldest brother, Devon, arrived home on foot, breathless and trembling. His words were barely audible. As he was driving home that night, he was stopped along the way by a group of people begging for a ride from Anse Garret to La Vieille Ville near Vigie. He complied and took them into his car. As he drove, the passengers laughed and talked among themselves. Devon intermittently joined in the conversation and shared their laughter. Suddenly, there was a pronounced silence in the car. Devon thought for a while: "Maybe they have all fallen asleep." Curiosity caused him to look around. He looked to his left and there was no one in the front seat. Then he peeped into the back seat, only to find that he was the lone occupant in the car. In fear, he parked the car and trusted his feet to take him home safely!

Too scared to be back on the road so soon even after his parents had helped him to retrieve his car, Devon had decided to stay at home the following night. Reminiscing over the event of the previous night, he recalled a similar experience with lesser impact on his nerves. Devon recalled going home one night when a cat scampered across his path and left him petrified. The morning after, he was met by a well-known little old hag in the community who stopped him and warned him: "'Next time do not stone animals in the night. You might just hurt somebody." Devon stopped short. He tried to see into her eyes but to no avail. He said, "The next time you cross my path, instead of being in your bed, I will kill you!" The old hag simply bowed her head and made off home.

The memories of Geckoville too rushed through his mind and reinforced the sequence of events which landed Carmen on her face at the expense of Ma Oliva's reputation. Flashbacks are torturous, but sometimes helpful, in that one leads to another to reinforce a situation through parallels and gives clarity to an immediate confrontational situation. This was the predicament in which Fr. Laport found himself. One thing led to another in the Carmen and Ma Oliva drama.

Not only did his childhood revisit him, but a similar experience was immediately brought back in sharp focus which made him more sympathetic towards Ma Oliva. It was Geckoville.

Did Fr. Laport stray from Solfatara Town? Did Devon, Dada, Dubois and Geckoville consume his thoughts? No! The drama of Solfatara Town, the home of sulfur and fire, that town where the sacred and profane live side by side and some saints and demons share a soul, was still far from over. Perhaps the experience of his brother, Devon, must have offered Fr. Laport some solace and encouragement for the way forward. The incident of Dada and Dubois in Geckoville served as a reassurance that Solfatara Town had her counterparts littered throughout all of Helen Island. Carmen's predicament only exhumed the past and afforded Fr. Laport an opportunity to piece the puzzle together. In other words, even if Ma Fano, Jablé and Dad had died, there were still many like Carmen who had not learned. The spirit they invoked continued to influence the lives of innocent people like Ma Oliva, Yvonne and Baby Joela.

Yvonne and Baby Joela

Yvonne lived on the outskirts of Solfatara Town. She was the proud mother of a little nine month old baby. Yvonne walked into Fr. Laport's office to register baby Joela for baptism. Baby Joela was full of energy. She was her mother's pride and joy more so since she was her mother's firstborn. Intermittently, baby Joela fixed her eyes on Fr. Laport's eyes and gave the usual baby smile and a giggle here and there. Unprovoked and for no particular reason, Fr. Laport whispered beneath his breath: "Jesus is Lord." His lips hardly moved. Each time he whispered the phrase, "Jesus is Lord," baby Joela went hysterical and dug her little fingernails into Yvonne's face. Whenever Fr. Laport stopped repeating the phrase, baby Joela was the most peaceful and loving baby one had ever seen. Poor Yvonne was livid at her baby's

46

behaviour. The young mother was clueless as to what was happening. At one time, Yvonne begged to be excused but Fr. Laport asked her to stay on a while longer. He convinced her that baby Joela was just being her natural self. All he wanted to do was to observe baby Joela a little longer.

Something was amiss, but what was it? 'A baby,' he said to himself, 'and she cannot tolerate the name of Jesus.' In all of this, Fr. Laport was cautious enough to say nothing that would alarm or intimidate Yvonne and, in turn, distance her from her baby. As the interview continued, Fr. Laport continued to monitor baby Joela's behaviour. The family showed up at baptism preparation classes. Every mention of the name, Jesus, sent baby Joela hysterical. Neither Yvonne nor anyone else in the family at the baptism preparation classes paid any attention to what was happening. When the baptism day arrived, Baby Joela was the most restless baby of the lot. It was only after the rite of exorcism had been performed over baby Joela that she went silent and fell into a deep sleep.

Fr. Laport looked at Yvonne and the family in total disbelief. He just could not understand how clueless the entire family had been all along. After Mass one Sunday morning, Fr. Laport decided to have a word with the family and to share a little of what he had observed. During the course of the conversation with the family, he learned that Patrick, baby Joela's father, had Joela initiated into a cult where she was dipped into a tub filled with water, incense, and an assortment of leaves. The tub was surrounded by an assortment of different coloured lighted candles while some prayers were recited from the Secret of the Psalms. "In whom or what was she initiated?" Fr. Laport asked the family. Their lips were sealed.

Yvonne blamed Patrick. Patrick blamed his father Harold. Harold in turn blamed his wife Beth. It was Beth who had advised them to take Joela and her parents to Ma Fano's house for Ma Fano to perform a rite of protection over Joela. "Ma Fano" Fr. Laport repeated out loud. "Yes, Father," Yvonne replied. "It is the same Ma Fano from Solfatara Town. The woman you *bouché* (caught red-handed) in her house, in her evil acts; it was she who did it for us." Fr. Laport's eyes danced in their sockets. His hands were raised "My God!" he shouted. "What on earth is wrong with you Catholics? Why can't you let God be God for you, just for once?" Then came the lame excuse, "We do not know any better. We are both young, we are inexperienced. We followed the directives of those who are older than we are. Besides, they are the *poto légliz* (pillars of the church) in the parish."

Fr. Laport hummed. It sounded like a lamentation. His heart was weeping. His efforts, he thought were all futile. Then Fr. Laport remembered that evangelization was a lifelong mission. He'd been in Solfatara Town for just a little over a year. Jesus spent three years proclaiming the Good News but he did not succeed in converting the Jews. Then how on earth did he expect to convert Solfatara Town in a year, if those who preceded him, did the best they could and had only just scratched the surface? What he did not understand was that Solfatara Town was only the bashing of the waves. The tsunami was still pending. He pondered for a while and wondered: which book do Catholics read from; it can't be the Bible?

Forbidden Books

Fr. Laport's mind had to come back to Solfatara Town. Like Jonah, his whale seemed more assured than the ship traversing the turbulent seas. Then his options for going in the opposite direction were growing thin. Instead, his destination to Nineveh looked more definite. There was still work to be done in Solfatara Town. As turbulent as the tides were, the sea was the only way across and Fr. Laport had no options left. He had to cross it.

While Fr. Laport was sitting peacefully in his office one afternoon, a young man walked in. The poor soul looked utterly ravaged. Fr.

Laport wondered for a while, 'Did he just come home from war?'
'Yes! But his war was waged on a different front, not with flesh and
blood as Fr. Laport would have preferred. If it were flesh and blood,
then it would have been a lot easier to counsel the young man. As
the young man took a seat before Fr. Laport's desk, he said, "Father,
I'm desperately in need of your help. For want of a better word, my
life is f.... messed up." He was about to use the "F" word when Fr.
Laport politely interrupted his flow of words. From the young man's
description of his life, he'd definitely been to hell and back; or perhaps
he had just been to hell itself. According to the young man, there was
not a book on the occult that he had not read. There were no spirits
in there that he had not invoked and there were no rituals that he
had not performed. Now he was in torment and pursued by what Fr.
Laport discerned to be more than six legions – judging by the young
man's description.

By then Fr. Laport felt paralyzed in his chair. The punch line of
the young man's story: "Father, believe me, last night I was directed
to go to the cemetery with a white fowl, tear its guts open and place
it over my head and let the blood flow over me. I was promised that
I would be redeemed but instead my woes have only increased." As
much as Fr. Laport felt great empathy for the young man, he felt that
his hands were tied at his back by the young man himself. The young
man verbally drove a ten inch nail into his own coffin with one simple
request: "Father, do for me whatever you can but do not ask me to
make any commitment to Jesus. Jesus is too demanding and I'm not
prepared to surrender my life to him." "In that case," said Fr. Laport
to the young man, "the door is all yours. Take it but do not let it hit
you in the butt on your way out."

Until then the name and publisher of the occult literature had
never been heard of by Fr. Laport. Of course curiosity bells the cat.
After the young man willingly obeyed his marching orders, Father
Laport lingered in his chair for a while, repeating in his mind the

name of the publisher over and over again. Suddenly he remembered an uncle who was like a confidant to him. There was no subject they could not discuss openly. He picked up the telephone and called, "Hey uncle what's up? What's cooking today?" From the other end of the line came the voice: "I'm here, what's cooking in the parish today?" "The usual parochial woes, I think," said Fr. Laport. "Without further ado, uncle, I want to run something by you. Are you ready for it?" "What's it? Run it by me! Let me see if I can be of any assistance to you." "Okay here it comes. What do you know about this publisher?" (Name withheld.) "'My God!" responded Fr. Laport's uncle, "What has prompted you to go there? Are you crossing over into the threshold of the demons? For heaven's sake, remember you are a priest! Look! What are you doing later this evening? Can I came over to see you and we'll discuss this a little further?" "Oh most definitely uncle, that's why I called you," replied Fr. Laport.

When Fr. Laport's uncle walked out of the door, unknowingly, he left his nephew a cache of weapons that evening. Little did his uncle know that he had given his nephew a fully charged grenade, well poised to set a massive explosion in the castles of the many Catholics posing as saints but dabbling in the forces of darkness. The following Sunday the congregation was on fire. Fr. Laport swore on the Pope's tomb that the effects of the evangelization were still being felt despite all else. People were still very much on fire. As someone put it, "There may be many people in church but not all are there for the same purpose and with the same agenda." Fr. Laport was about to discover that truism on that Sunday.

That fateful Sunday was a turning point for the masqueraders in the flock posing as sheep although they were foxes and wolves. Fr. Laport was like a firebrand. He never minced his words. His mouth was like a river without any stones and every thought had free expression. Whatever he delivered that morning was in keeping with the above description of his tongue and mouth. To this day, many people are not sure how to describe it: a sermon or a serpent? Whichever way one may choose to describe it, its sting was like that of a serpent. It sent many persons running for cover at the end of Mass. Fr. Laport named all the books which he knew at that time were published by the known publishers. He asked the children to look out for them at home and if any were found, then people would know on which side of the fence certain members of the family stood or sat.

By Jove! When Mass ended that Sunday there was a desperate rush. Some individuals left behind spouse and children even if it meant returning to meet them later. By midmorning, Solfatara Town was like a furnace and smoke was bellowing from every quarter. Bonfires were everywhere. By Monday morning the name, Fr. Laport, in Solfatara Town was like a bad omen. Indeed a war had just begun and the town's aristocrats were furious at having to hurriedly burn their treasured books before family members discovered them. One man was caught red handed with the "Sixth and Seventh Books of Moses" and was repeatedly accused of sorcery and Black Magic. He told Fr. Laport that if one wanted to be a man in today's world, he must first learn to protect himself. "You are talking about wealth and power here," the man added. Above all the man was livid. Solfatara Town had been struck a fatal blow that morning. A travesty above all travesties had been committed by Fr. Laport that fateful Sunday. The dabblers and followers of the occult felt Fr. Laport had "desecrated" the altar.

Later that week Fr. Laport was invited to the Chancery Office to answer to the Archbishop for the travesty he had committed. He was accused of breaking down family trust, desecrating the altar and abusing the powers afforded him in the pulpit. Those offended expected an immediate public apology. Such charges and demands Fr. Laport found both ridiculous and absurd. Nevertheless, he said that a man is free to justify his conscience and maintain his integrity before men, even if it was at the expense of his own salvation. However, having endured his baptism in the turbulent waters thus far, he too was prepared to stand his ground and hold firm to his convictions. There was no room for lukewarm or hypocritical Christians in the kingdom of God. Christians, he believed, had made a vow to God: "I renounce the devil and all his works and promises and I give myself to Jesus through the hands of Mary." To violate this vow and to return to the very things that were renounced, year in and year out, was nothing but a serious malaise of the soul and a farce without parallel, "What an unnecessary encumbrance for anyone to impose upon himself and, at the same time, to make the lives of others a living hell and to impede the growth of the Church," said Fr. Laport.

The Archbishop, like a gentle and humble father to his priest, started his meeting with Fr. Laport on a very jovial note. They shared some delightful moments on their pastoral ministries. Then the Archbishop listened attentively as Fr. Laport shared his side of the story concerning the reports he had received. Amazed by what Fr. Laport communicated to him, in comparison with the reports he had received, the Archbishop thought it wise to have a word with Fr. Fallon, the Pastor, for verification's sake. Then and there the Archbishop took the telephone, dialed and made immediate contact with Fr. Fallon. The two spoke for about ten minutes. Intermittently there were outbursts of laughter while they spoke on the telephone. When the telephone conversation ended, the Archbishop picked up the conversation where he had left off with Fr. Laport. At the end of the meeting, the Archbishop commented: "As your Bishop, I share your enthusiasm and your zeal. As a young priest there are always allowances made for error. You may have to choose the appropriate forum to divulge certain information." The Archbishop neither judged nor condemned Fr. Laport. In the most humble way he suggested to him that prudence is better than a cure. Next time, be outspoken but in the right forum. On this note the meeting ended and Fr. Laport returned to Solfatara Town hoping that he would swim against the turbulent waves, not in the belly of a whale, but with God as his guide. However, what you hope for and what befalls you are not the same if you are destined to be another Job. For while even God took a rest on the seventh day and Jesus repeatedly cautioned his disciples to do the same, the devil's day must have been thirty-six hours long and his week must have exceeded seven days. The devil never rested. He assumes as many personas as there are available to manifest his presence and his way in the life of humankind. The *Boloms* are a typical example.

One night, just as the clock struck midnight, a voice which sounded like that of an infant was heard weeping and wailing outside of the Chapel of Repose. Even the ears of those who were deep in prayer were not deaf to the distracting cry. An elderly gentleman stepped outside quietly and made his way into the yard to see what was happening. His re-entry into the chapel was like a catapult band receding after the release of its projectile. Breathless as he was, he mumbled beneath his struggling breath in Kwéyòl: *"an bolom."* A *bolom* in Helenite tradition is said to be a living fetus extracted involuntarily from the womb of its mother, kept in a bottle in some dark place during the day but allowed to roam at night under the direction of its master to perform specific tasks. Was the *bolom* misdirected that night? The answer is still a mystery.

Two days later, while Fr. Laport was conducting a Bible Study class at an outstation about eight miles from Assumption, a contingent arrived at Sts. Monica and Augustine's Church. They had travelled from the neighbouring parish of St. John Vianney, eight miles to the north of Solfatara and were directed by Fr. Fallon to find Fr Laport there. They carried with them an erratic little four year old girl who was seeing something but could not put it into words. She was indeed hysterical! Fr. Laport simply asked those who were attending the Bible Study to turn their gaze to the Blessed Sacrament and pray the

Holy Rosary on his behalf and that of the little girl. He then prayed over and blessed the little girl for about half an hour after which she suddenly fell into a deep sleep. Her family and friends took her back home. The dark days and nights seemed like a never ending stream. Silently in his heart, Fr. Laport prayed to God and asked, "Lord, when will it end? When will I leave Solfatara Town?" Fr. Laport learnt one simple lesson after this prayer, "Be very careful what you ask of God' for no one knows the answer God has in mind.

Goodbye Solfatara Town

It was not too long after Father Laport had prayed and asked the Lord to take him away from Solfatara Town that his prayer was answered. One Sunday afternoon, Fr. Laport was alone at home. He was in his office preparing his Religious Education class for the following day. The telephone rang, "Hello!" At the other end the voice answered: "Fr. Laport, it's the Archbishop. I'm visiting the sisters next door. Do you have a minute? I'll be stopping by." "Okay, Your Grace, I will await your arrival." Minutes later the Archbishop was at Fr. Laport's office door. Fr. Laport greeted the Archbishop at the door and they both proceeded into Fr. Laport's office. Quite an animated conversation ensued between them, interrupted by sporadic laughter.

Towards the end of the visit, the Archbishop stared Fr. Laport in the face and said, "For your own safety, I think the time has come when we should transfer you to another parish. My preference for you is at Conception in Félicitéville." "Félicitéville! Oh no, Your Grace! I'll go anywhere else but not Félicitéville," Fr. Laport protested. With the voice of a compassionate father, the Archbishop interrupted and said, "Give it a try. We'll see what happens. Think about it and give me call."

After the Archbishop departed, Fr. Laport slumped into his chair and reached for his Jerusalem Bible and opened it. There his eyes fell on the passage, "I tell you solemnly, when you were young you put on your own belt and walked where you liked; but when you grow old you will stretch out your hands, and somebody will put a belt round you and take you where you would rather not go. (John 21:18)." The Lord had spoken with abundant clarity. What else could Fr. Laport have said if not, "I will go to Félicitéville". Would his past in Solfatara Town follow him into Félicitéville? Time would tell. Fr. Laport had a saying: A priest is a nomad. Those who greet him should always ask, "Where are you?" before asking, "how you are?" The time had come to depart to embrace a new vision. Fr. Laport was at that point optimistic that Félicitéville held the key to a brighter vision and for a better pastorate. He was convinced by then that he had graduated. Solfatara Town was his university. He was prepared to handle any new and pending challenges, but not another bout with spirits and witches.

Chapter Four

Félicitéville

Félicitéville was Fr. Laport's home parish. He owed his all to Conception Church. He was born on the outskirts of Félicitéville and still has his roots there. He received all the sacraments of initiation at Conception Church and was ordained to the Diaconate and Priesthood there as well. It is his wish to bid the world farewell from this same address.

Working in Félicitéville was like working in his backyard. There is an axiom, "A prophet is never respected in his own country and by his own people." Just the thought of this axiom was enough to cause much apprehension for Fr. Laport. Like a stuck disc, the same note kept playing over and over again in his head: 'I'm sent to be a prophet to my own people and my own household.' As the events of his ministry played out, he experienced just the opposite of his fears. Although he had the support of his family and his townspeople, the other concern was interference on the part of his family in his pastoral duties but that did not materialize. He had the support of the people and that made his stay in Félicitéville a lot easier.

Despite being loved by family and parishioners, Fr. Laport's reputation as an exorcist had preceded him. Of course that was the last thing he wanted to be known for. This was not a role one assumed on his own volition. It is an office bestowed on a particular priest by the local Bishop, the Ordinary of the diocese. Much as he tried to shy away from the responsibility, his parishioners made heavy demands upon him in this regard. Consequently, his honeymoon in Félicitéville at Conception was short-lived and the turbulent waters began threatening to sweep him off his feet once again.

Sooner than he had expected, Fr. Laport was inundated with calls for appointments to visit homes and meet persons who were allegedly victims of spirits and demons. In his own mind he argued with himself, 'Wasn't I given a transfer from Solfatara Town to Félicitéville for my own safety?' Of course the argument was all rhetorical; it had no merit and would give him no consolation. Why? No member of the Church hierarchy or any member of the clergy or even family and friends were privy to his private thoughts and inner struggles, other than his personal confessor. In fact, he never intended to divulge such information to anyone else. One thing Fr. Laport was very conscious of in all of this was his own human inadequacy. He often wondered how he was able to survive Solfatara Town. The question before him now was: "Will I survive Félicitéville?" Despite his fears, Fr. Laport had understood that with God at his side, he had survived Solfatara Town. Therefore, he had the faith to believe that he would survive Félicitéville.

Félicitéville had its pros and cons. It was the capital of Helen Island. Hence, Fr. Laport presupposed that the people there would be of a different ilk. Often those from Félicitéville frowned on the folks from the countryside and suburban areas, reckoning them as "country bookies". This meant that there were certain traits, patterns of behaviour and traditions among the country folk that were not too readily accepted by the city dwellers. The city dwellers on the other hand considered themselves prim and proper in all ways. Many considered that they were the middle class or the aristocrats. Truth be told: it was all a myth.

Fr. Laport, very early, discovered that Helenites were Helenites regardless of the city, town, village or country they lived in or migrated to. You could move a Helenite out of Helen Island but couldn't remove the "Heleniteness" from them. Their consciousness was shaped by their culture and environment which went way beyond the borders of Helen Island itself and the mere physical location of their flesh and bones. In other words, every human person is a shadow of his or her ancestors. Every living person is for Fr. Laport, a mere shadow of a distant past, journeying through time and adapting to social and spiritual demands of the cultural environment which shape his or her consciousness. Each person therefore bring out of his treasure things both old and new. Sometimes, the old and the new are not always well understood and maybe even irreconcilable but that's the law of human nature.

Helenites are predominantly the descendants of black Africans. For them, like their African ancestors, the spirit world is just as real as the world of flesh and blood. Any phenomena beyond human explanation are immediately and directly attributed to the works of the spirits. Fr. Laport would discover that there are more demons in the mind than there are in the soul, or even the body of the afflicted. This calls for a great deal of discernment lest everyone embarks on a journey chasing demons from behind every tree. Most demons are the creative imagination of some pernicious minds. Others are creatures of human creation brought to birth by willful defiance of the rubrics of natural law in pursuance of selfish motives towards the attainment of wants at the expense of salvation and peace of mind. Greed and idolatry are inseparable and they open doors and windows of the soul for entry of the devil.

Still some demons do exist but are invoked by men and women with malevolent habits who live for the purpose of casting maledictions on the lives of their unsuspecting neighbours.

Fr. Laport contends, regardless of the classification, some demons are human creations and the consequences of human misjudgments. Strange but true, Fr. Laport noted that demons and demonic beliefs are without class distinctions: country bookie, middle class and aristocrats all believed in the existence of demons and demon possession, especially in Helen Island. Heraldin is a typical case in point.

Heraldin

Heraldin, laboured at snail pace into Fr. Laport's office. Her face was battered; her eyes all swollen, her speech slurred, and her bloated frame looked laced by heavy doses of sedatives. The poor young lady kept munching away like a cow. Between every word she uttered was a loud disturbing belch. Occasionally, she spoke in the voice of various persons and acted out various personalities. All of this gave one the distinct conviction that Heraldin was indeed possessed. Both she and her parents, were convinced that she was possessed, since of course, she showed all the symptoms of one who was possessed. "She was in a sorry state," recounted Fr. Laport.

Memories of Solfatara town were revisiting Fr. Laport but he was determined not to let his mistakes revisit him as well. He was not prepared for any high drama. It had been a year since he was ordained and it was time to show wisdom in thinking and in actions even more so in pastoral duties and responsibilities. After a lengthy interview with Heraldin and her parents, Fr. Laport decided to schedule another meeting with Heraldin the following week, giving him as much time as possible to pray over the situation. When Heraldin and her parents left his office, Fr. Laport was convinced, for some unknown reason, that something was amiss. Not only was the conversation analogous to some drama he had seen before but there seemed to be a lot more ambiguities in the demeanour of the parents, in particular, her father.

The mind is as deceptive to the body as it is destructive to the soul. Like a sleeping policeman, one can ride over it but never penetrate it unless, out of necessity, it is analysed for repairs or total removal. It was mere drudgery trying to penetrate Heraldin's mind to unearth the cause of her predicament. Her parents wanted to lend her their voices even though she was old enough to speak for herself. Did they have a hidden agenda? Were they trying to conceal something? Fr. Laport was left to wonder.

For more than three months, Fr. Laport worked with Heraldin until finally, with her parents out of the room, she surrendered to the light from the forces of darkness which held her in a siege. This darkness had made her a walking zombie, manifesting the behaviour of a cow and causing her to live in a sedated state. For the first time since her early childhood, she threw open the door of her prison cell to breathe, the fresh air of a prisoner just placed on parole. Heraldin was the victim of incest.

Her demons did not originate from the dark world of principalities and powers but from within what should have been the sanctuary of the family. When her temple was repeatedly violated and desecrated over and over again, Heraldin's mind became her demon. She was living in an imaginary Ghostville. Self-esteem eluded her. Figuratively, she repeatedly hid herself in the body of an imaginary cow. This cow was her protective cover. 'No one, in their right senses, except one who is a zoophile would derive erotic fixation with her body under such conditions,' she thought. She was misguided. Her abuser knew exactly how to decode her defence mechanisms. She was his victim simply because of her sex. Her personhood had no meaning to him in spite of the fact that he was duty bound to honour her and respect her, as the scriptures required her to honour him that she might have long life in the land of the living.

Her defence mechanisms were manifold. Each day she had no option but to adopt a new identity. This was the only way Heraldin could cope with this deep dark secret. Heraldin lived between the devil and the deep blue sea. She was told that the day she divulged the dark secret, she would never see the light of day again. As the days turned into months and the months turned into years, she took refuge in her infancy, which made her believe it was only a game. Her defences were all useless in the face of her abuser who never recognised that he was her demon. Instead, he made others believe that his daughter was insane and that, according to the fortune-teller, a witch who lived next door had put a hex on her.

He was her demon: a pedophile and zoophile in one – the demon that never recognised his own demons, while searching for demons in those he had demonized. Did her violator, her abuser, and his cohort ever realize they were her demons? Did they ever reckon that the demons whom they insisted must be cast out of Heraldin, were mere phantoms generated by pernicious habits which they tried so desperately to conceal?

The Souls of the Unborn

At the end of this disturbing drama, Fr. Laport over and over again asked himself, "Am I a ghost hunter?" His name and his ministry had become synonymous with ghosts, spirits and disturbances in the minds of his congregation. It was not a position or a title or an office he enjoyed at all, but he understood his priesthood as a call to liberating souls and preparing them for the Kingdom of God. He understood then, that like his Lord and Master, he had a calling to redeem souls from their distress. Out of love, he was duty bound to be a servant of divine mercy. Even in that frame of mind, Fr. Laport knew he still had to rely on divine providence and God's wisdom to guide him so that he would judge every case on its own merit.

At the sound of the slightest disturbance at any home, people called at his office. He was convinced that if some measure of control was not put in place, he would be nicknamed: "Father Ghost Hunter". Certainly, he was not prepared to embrace such a title. He was determined to put an end to it before the situation got out of hand. He thought people had to recognise where they had failed and how much they too were responsible for their suffering and hours of despair.

After much prayer and reflection, it was revealed to Fr. Laport that if the souls of the dead were not put to rest, this could have some serious implications in each case for the peace and well-being of the living. Fr. Laport pondered on the descriptions of the disturbances in the homes, the shadows cast against the walls and the visions that families had to endure both days and nights. Quietly in his heart, Fr. Laport prayed, "Lord, put into my heart and mind the most suitable approach to handle these revelations. Let your Holy Spirit guide me through this. I need your wisdom."

From that moment onwards, whenever Fr. Laport was invited to bless a home or a family with such problems, he took time off to interview the family members and took a journey with them into their lives and their lifestyles. He never blessed a home under such conditions unless he had heard the family story. Fr. Laport thought it wise to have a chat with the family, particularly so, when the family thought they were seeing ghosts darting across their living rooms and bedrooms and their infants engaged in imaginary conversations with ghosts.

One day while on a home visit, Fr. Laport listened attentively to the woes of a family who had not slept a wink for a while. Their baby daughter cried ceaselessly through the night, night after night. They were at their wits' end. Fr. Laport asked to speak privately with the mother of the house. His question to her was straight and direct, "Have you ever had any abortions?" Shocked out of her wits, her eyes narrowed and ruts and ridges grew out of her forehead. After much hesitation, she asked, "Father, why are you asking such a personal question?" "Because," said Fr. Laport, "the souls of the unborn and the unbaptized will not rest until the living put them to rest. Chances are they will disturb the living too." Her eyes and shoulders fell in tandem, and under her breath she mumbled, "Yes Father, two." Fr. Laport responded, "Give them a name. We'll call their souls and send them back to the Lord. Will you, accept baptism on their behalf?" Fr. Laport asked. "Yes," she said. Fr. Laport instructed the mother and other family members on the procedure and then conducted the rites.

At the anointing, from nowhere, on either side of the mother, came the pungent aroma of freshly picked lilies, strong enough to alert the attention of everyone in the sitting room. Everyone turned in the direction of the aroma but said nothing, except that question marks were hanging on every face: *'What on earth is happening here?'*

When all was said and done, Fr. Laport asked, "Did something disturb you guys?" The response was unanimous: "Yes, Father, like fresh lilies! What was that?" "The souls of the unborn," Father replied. Unanimously they cried, "Really!" "Yes, they are redeemed; there is no need to fear." The home was blessed and all disturbances ceased. However, Fr. Laport was quick to caution the family: "Always be slow to condemn your neighbours. Like Frankenstein, we create our own monsters. Sadly though, we do not see them and so we can't dismantle the structures they build around us. Instead they chew at our lives, sometimes to the point of death. Look deep into your closets before you blame your neighbour for what you have created for yourselves."

Mervina

Up until now, Félicitéville, unlike Solfatara Town, had been extremely hospitable to Fr. Laport. He had a honeymoon he'd never had in Solfatara Town. To the best of his ability, he enjoyed every moment of it and prayed that God would leave it just that way. However, that was not meant to be. The same Satan, who visited the land of Job and devastated Job out of malice and jealousy, must have been just an earshot away.

It was literally the next day when an angel came, not with good news but with the contrary. For Fr. Laport, she was the bearer of bad news. He was happy to see her. He greeted her, "Angel of God, what good news hast thou brought with thee?" She raised her eyebrow and said nervously, "Fa, Fa, Father we need your help." "Help for what?"

"Father," she continued, "there is a young lady I'd like you to visit with us. She's having a dusty time." "What's the matter with her?" he asked. Fumbling over her words, she stuttered, "I, I, I think they said she is possessed. But she is a lovely girl who works in my office." Fr. Laport's hope for a long peace was dashed. His eyes searched Angel's face for a reason why she had turned to him. There were other priests: Fr. Paul, the Administrator, Frs. Chris and Antipas; they were all Frs. Laport's seniors. The more he searched her face, the more her face betrayed her thoughts, *'Linger as you will, hesitate as you must, but we will set a date for an appointment to see Mervina.'*

Finally, Fr. Laport broke his silence.'

"Will you bring her to my office?" he asked. "No Father! I think it would be better to see her at home due to the nature of the case." At the mention of the nature of the case, Fr. Laport's suspicions were more than his mind could bear. Instantly he had a flashback to Solfatara Town and he broke into a cold sweat. However, that did not let him off the hook. "Saturday, shall we say," was her persistent quest for a date. Fr. Laport, out of compassion for Angel, and more so for Mervina, acceded to Angel's request and agreed to Saturday at nine-thirty in the morning.

On Saturday morning, armed with his stole, Bible, holy water and blessed salt, Fr. Laport, Angel and Angel's team of prayer warriors arrived at Mervina's house. The place looked eerie. The yard was littered with chickens. A few cats loitered lazily across the yard as if performing an involuntary ritual. Their heads were drooping to the ground as if they were downcast and hated the fact that the sun had risen too early and their prey had receded to their hiding place and had left them without a catch. The three dogs lying at the door did not care whether the visitors were friends, thieves or foes. They never winked, never moved. It looked like they had ended their night watch. They were exhausted and were too happy to see dawn. Subsequently, they allowed nothing to disturb their morning's rest.

As soon as Fr. Laport, Angel and her team stepped into the sitting room, Angel and her team burst into a litany of songs and prayers. Mervina sauntered out of the room, as if bewildered to see a priest and whole group of people taking her house by storm. She was disheveled, her eyes dazed, and her face set like ten rat traps. Rags must have been her uniform for the day. In the hail of songs, prayers and praise, Fr. Laport greeted Mervina who mumbled under her breath "Morning Father." "How are you doing today?" Father asked. "Fine," she answered briskly. Her responses all sounded like, "What the hell are you people doing in my house?" Fr. Laport gathered that either Angel did not inform Mervina of their coming, or it may have slipped Mervina's mind altogether.

Despite the hostile reception, Fr. Laport, for the sake of peace, decided to bless the home before he could sit with Mervina for a heart to heart talk. At that point, was this the best thing to do? Was he sufficiently informed of what he had accepted to undertake? It did not seem so. It looked like Fr. Laport had more on his plate than he had bargained for and would be able to eat in one sitting. Just as Fr. Laport raised his hand and the first drops of holy water reached across the room, Father felt himself thrown headlong in the opposite direction. He hardly had time to catch his breath and to understand what exactly had happened. There was an instantaneous unrehearsed chorus of clucking chickens. Desperately they fled to safety. The cats and dogs too went berserk: the dogs howled; the cats forgot their lethargic stroll, gathered as much momentum as they could and scampered to safety under a nearby chicken coup where they took refuge. From there, their eyes glittered in the semidarkness.

As for Angel and her group of ladies, they held their note until all the commotion had died down. Then they continued on the exact note as if they had never been interrupted at all. As for Fr. Laport, his blood must have stopped flowing through his veins. "I'm a priest" he told himself. "I must be a person of faith for the others." Gathering his strength and his breath, he took a seat opposite Mervina at the far end of the verandah. From there he conducted an interview with her before proceeding any further. He realized that he was dealing with a force which seemed much bigger than himself. Even the atmosphere, too, in the room had changed drastically among the ladies. Their trepidation was evident. The discomfort among the women who prayed could have been felt from miles away, without exaggeration. Fr. Laport, slowly adjusted to the situation. His plate was full. His dinner had to be eaten in many courses if he was to clean up all that was set before him.

Moreover, Fr. Laport understood, after being thrown across the room by what eyes could not see and hands could not touch, that he did not come up against flesh and blood. Also, in this case, he could not call the authorities. It was completely out of the question to rely on any physical strength, force or man-made weaponry. All were useless for this battle. What he needed at that critical moment were true soldiers of Jesus Christ. His foot soldiers were weakened by the experience. Their lips quivered, even as they prayed, and their fingers twitched nervously and literally. Their voices showed signs of weariness.

Even with all these signs of trepidation and recognizing the magnitude of what they were dealing with, Fr. Laport had the temerity to ask Angel to increase their prayer power. "Pray the Holy Rosary," he told them. "Let your hearts and mind be one in prayer. Do not let there be any weakening on your part." As the prayer power increased, Fr. Laport stood at a distance, not daring to lay hands on Mervina. He prayed the prayer of exorcism. This time it looked as if he had just stirred up a hornet's nest. The animals in the yard sounded as if they were individually stabbed each time holy water was sprinkled. Each time, another commotion ensued among the animals out in the yard. At the end of the prayer session, all was calm again but the chickens, cats and dogs all looked like they were still on edge. A mere shadow would agitate them again. Whatever happened to Mervina after the exorcism was to remain a mystery, since Angel never brought up her name again. Even when she was asked, the question was quickly avoided.

Not too long after the Mervina drama, a sheet of weariness draped Fr. Laport and landed him in the hospital. His Pastor blamed it all on stress, and thought it was best to have an exchange of priests between Helen Island and Nevis. Fr. Arthur willingly accepted the offer of working in Helen Island for two weeks and Fr. Laport was happy to extricate himself from the turbulent waters and to embrace a period of smooth sailing on calmer water. Indeed it was a time of peace, tranquility and prayer.

He was in Nevis, sitting on the verandah of the presbytery, deep in prayer, when, without any warning, Fr. Laport's mind drifted on a journey of its own. While on this journey, Fr. Laport saw himself preaching in a deep valley on arid ground and amidst mountains stripped of their vegetation. Gathering his thoughts, he wondered, *'What could that mean? Where is this godforsaken place?'* The more he tried to dismiss the thoughts of it, the more it seemed that the image of the place was etched into his mind. Try as he might, thoughts of this place haunted him until his return to Helen Island and Conception Church.

Goodbye Félicitéville

On his return to Helen Island, the power in Félicitéville was out. Assumption was plunged into darkness. Candles dimly lit the stairway up to his room. Just above one of the lighted candles hung a blackboard on which house notes were scribbled. There in bold letters read: "Fr. Laport, please contact Archbishop Francis immediately upon arrival." His heart skipped a beat. "I'm in trouble," he told himself. His luggage was barely off his hands when he grabbed the telephone and dialed the Archbishop's home number. After one ring a voice answered, "Hello, hello!" "Hey! Your Holiness, Fr. Laport here." "Fr. Laport," the Archbishop shouted as if with a sigh of relief. "I heard you were returning today and I have been awaiting your call!" "Am I in trouble or something, your Holiness?" The Archbishop laughed. "No! But can you come over to my office first thing in the morning. We'll have a chat." "Okay, Your Holiness, I'll see you in the morning. Have a good night."

At nine o' clock Fr. Laport arrived at the Chancery and was ushered into the Archbishop's office. The greeting was cordial as ever. After a quick chit-chat, it was down to business. First the Archbishop lavished his thanks and gratitude upon Fr. Laport for his dedicated pastoral ministry as an assistant in Solfatara Town and Félicitéville. Amidst the thanks and gratitude expressed, Fr. Laport remained dumb. He just did not know in which direction the conversation was going. Without any warning, Fr. Laport was being handed his marching orders out of Félicitéville to be Acting Pastor of Potsville and Bay-of-Ray. Taken by surprise by the quick change of events, he said to the Archbishop, "I am a young priest with little experience and you are not giving me a parish. Instead you are handing me a diocese: two parishes eight miles apart. How am I going to handle this?" "We will guide you; God will direct you and the parishioners will assist you." The Archbishop ended the meeting by thanking Fr. Laport for graciously accepting his assignments, perhaps totally or partly unaware of how apprehensive the poor man was.

Chapter Five

Potsville and Bay-of-Ray

T he date of the appointment had arrived. Fr. Laport assumed responsibility as an Acting Pastor for the first time. He took up residence in Potsville and administered Bay-of-Ray from there. The geographical layout and social environment of Bay-of-Ray had something peculiar about it. Even while in transit through Bay-of-Ray, there was an eerie feeling about it. For a while Fr. Laport thought to himself: 'It was only something subconscious on his part. Perhaps it was just his prejudice, due in part, to the physical layout of Bay-of-Ray.' Try as much as he did, Father Laport could not discern whether it was just a mental attitude or a downright personal prejudice against Bay-of –Ray. He just could not fathom it. When he did express his feelings and experiences to others, it was as if he were speaking a foreign language. Fr. Laport felt heavily restricted and inhibited during his sermons. He complained that he carried a heavy weight on his chest and was not comfortable delivering as he did in other parishes. For a time he paid it no mind and concentrated on the way forward, trying to share his time between Potsville and Bay-of-Ray.

Bay-of-Ray never slept. The people there took it in turn to sleep. All night long there was a hustle and bustle and sometimes a tussle or two before the night was over. They were a people of faith. They came to church in large numbers but for many, the spirit of Denros Bounty Rum, which was readily available, at a price, was more enticing than that of the Holy Spirit who is a free gift to all who asked for it. In short, Bay-of-Ray could only offer what it had: sleeplessness. She was not Fr. Laport's sweetheart at all. He loved his sleep.

Potsville was the opposite. By seven or eight o'clock at night her streets could have been named *Ghost Avenue*. It was mainly on weekends when the competing discos vied for clients but some people, who lived in close proximity to the noise, longed for the peace and quiet of dawn. The presbytery was nicely perched on a hillside and away from the din of it all. However, it was not exempted from the hum of the intermittent traffic flow. It was in search of a peaceful night's rest that Fr. Laport made Potsville his place of residence. Whether he had spent a day or an afternoon in Bay-of-Ray at sunset, Fr. Laport made his way back to Potsville. Was that a safe thing for Fr. Laport? Only time would tell.

Whether it was late night or the late evening, no matter what time it was after dark, whenever Fr. Laport made his way back to Potsville from Bay-of-Ray, he encountered a strange dog in a most isolated spot. Initially, he paid it no heed. "After all it is the nature of dogs to stray and this one was no exception," he thought. As time went by, Fr. Laport's suspicion strayed to where he thought it would never have strayed. He argued with himself as he drove along alone. Question after question raced through his mind. Why? There was something different, something unusual about that dog, something that did not quite add up. Why in the same spot, the same vicinity all the time? Was he guarding someone? For fear that he was diagnosed as being cynical, Fr. Laport maintained his silence until one evening, when dusk and night were still greeting each other and a glimmer of light lingered. This time Fr. Laport and his cousin were heading to Potsville.

Just as his car came round the bend, he spotted the dog walking down to its usual spot. His cousin asked, "Why is this little girl walking in a lonely and godforsaken place all by herself at this hour?" "Which little girl are you talking about?" Fr. Laport asked. Pointing in the direction of the dog, his cousin said, "This one." "How do you know it is a bitch?" Fr. Laport asked. "My God," his cousin replied.

"How can you refer to a person in that way?" his cousin asked. "Look closely," said Fr. Laport, "can't you see it's a dog for heaven's sake!" As the car approached the dog, his cousin wiped his eyes and said, "It's really a dog for true!" Finally, without warning, Fr. Laport pulled the car to a halt, stepped out and confronted the dog face to face.

He verbally threatened the dog, "If at anytime you cross my path again, I will give you a solid beating. I know you are not a dog. You are a person and soon I'll find out who you are." At that time, goose bumps grew like mushrooms on the skin of Fr. Laport and his cousin. On re-entering the car, his cousin chastised him for being so ridiculous to take such great risk with his life. "You have no idea what you are dealing with. Do you?" 'Nope! Not really," was his reply. "Who were you trying to impress?" "Not you. Not me. Not anyone. At least if it's really a dog, I'll meet it again tomorrow. But if it's not, guess what? Not you. Not me. No one else will ever see it again." Like two children they quibbled over each other's fears and idiosyncrasies until they got home and buried the hatchet.

The evening of the next day, at Mass, in his homily at Bay-of-Ray, Fr. Laport shared his experience of the previous night with the congregation. In the course of his delivery, a little old lady quickly glided beneath the pews and squeezed her way out of the church, complaining that the priest was accusing her of witchcraft. In colloquial terms she was a *Jan Gajé*. Sorry! There was no name calling. No individual had been singled out either. Just reference to what had happened the previous evening. A youth sitting at the back of the church near the entrance witnessed all that had taken place and she had heard the comments of the old lady. She, in Kwéyòl, commented out loud, *"Madam si i tonbé an jaden'w sèklé'y. Si lakou'w sal balyé'y."* In other words, "Woman, if you see your faults in those remarks, repent! There is no need to complain. If your life is out of sync with the homily, make amends." The little old lady went away quickly, as silently as a mouse.

In a matter of minutes, the news had reached the four corners of Bay-of-Ray. Before long there was a spectacle outside her door. People were shouting: *"Oswè-a nou ka bouché'w ou paka alé pyès koté."* (Tonight you are under siege, you cannot go out). There was a carnival atmosphere at her door. According to the tone of the conversation in the midst of this *mêlée,* the little old lady had long been suspected of witchcraft. Repeatedly, before this event, the boys on the block called her *Gajé,* but no one took it seriously. This time, by her guilty response and by a mere slip of the tongue, she had made a public confession without recognizing it. She had left herself exposed to the mercy of the villagers. After that night neither dog nor little girl was ever seen or found in that area again but the little old lady became Fr. Laport's bitter enemy for life.

Murder in Bay-of-Ray

Within weeks, the most uncivilized, most gruesome murder was committed in broad daylight in the streets of Bay-of-Ray. A young man by the name of Roland had appeared both erratic and disillusioned for a while. On that fateful day, Roland, like a wild leopard sprang from his hiding place and, leapt onto a man's back, threw him to the ground, bashed in his head with a rock and sucked the brain of the dying man through an opening he had made in his skull. The limbs of those who witnessed the crime felt like jellyfish. Fear and surprise at both the swiftness with which the young man sprang from the nearby bushes and the limited time that he took to bash the skull of his victim, left all paralyzed and helpless.

A wild fire was raging. The rumour mills were grinding. The *tell-a-person communication* lines were overloaded. The news of the gruesome murder was everywhere. Dismay seized the entire village. From neighbouring communities people were calling in to express their consternation and consolation. In Bay-of-Ray, fear had gripped every heart, mind and spirit causing a prolonged paralysis.

The stench of death hung over Bay-of-Ray like a hammer of justice. Roland was still sitting on the chest of his victim. His mouth stuck to his victim's head draining whatever was left of his brains. He was like a vampire. Everyone in the crowd kept a safe distance. No one dared to approach or ask him to stop. All thought alike: "Who would be his next victim?" Silence and consternation transfixed the crowd. The scene was a zone of silence. It was not out of respect for the dead. It was out of dread of the assailant. However, the dread of Roland never deterred more curious onlookers. It was when the police squad arrived with all their military gear that the crowd became rambunctious. Silence fled into the hills and the power of speech returned.

Roland was quickly identified as the grandson of the little old lady whose house was under siege after a public confession a few weeks earlier. A spectator in the crowd shouted, *"Ma Claratine sé gwanmanmany'y. Tibway-a modi! Claratine, yo di vole batem'y, èk tè van lam'y bay demou.* In other words: "He is the grandson of Ma Claratine. The boy is cursed! His grandmother allegedly stole his baptism. She sold his soul to the devil." On a more sympathetic note, some people said the young man was not culpable. "Ma Claratine is fully responsible for his actions. She had no right to steal his baptism and sell his soul to the devil. The devil took possession of his soul and made him commit such a gruesome crime," they said.

"The priests too must accept their fair share of blame. They must be more careful and selective in their choice of candidates to serve as godparents." An elderly gentleman in the crowd boldly admitted: "That's true! Everybody in Bay-of-Ray knows Ma Claratine is a witch. How come Fadda don't know that? You mean she had to block Fadda Laport on the road before he knows? I wonder what the church teaching them priests at the seminary?" Another gentleman took him up on his statement: "How come is Fr. Laport you holding responsible for this situation? The priest is a young priest. I'm sure he does not know a thing of what just happen there." That was the end of the verbal exchange. The subject met its untimely death.

The boisterous crowd, on the other hand, carried on unrestrained for a long while. The assailant, Roland, was taken into custody first at the village Police Station and later to Félicitéville Police Station. In the midst of the sweltering heat and the collective body heat of the crowd, everyone was drenched in sweat. The air got thicker and thicker every second. The larger the crowd grew, the more intense was the humidity. In their state of agitation people hardly paid attention to temperature as they spoke *ad-lib* about the predicament of the assailant and the unsuspecting victim. "The poor man," they lamented, "met an untimely death in a brutal manner." The last straw to break the camel's back in the midst of all the *mêlée* was a teenager in the crowd who shouted: "All you Catholics are hypocrites. You are serving two masters. Now pay for your sins!" An elderly man shouted back in Kwéyòl, *"Sé pa Katolic tousèl ki ni vis. Lot Sé wilizyon ka fè zafè yo anba fèy."* In other words: "Catholics are not the only hypocrites. The other religions are very secretive in their doings."

In all of this, both the heavens and earth responded with sadness. Lightning struck like a rod of correction. Peals of thunder roared through the sky. The clouds grew thicker by the second. In the crowd a Rastaman kept posing at every streak of lightning. He claimed: "Jah taking I man photo!" An old man shouted at him: *"Sakwé kouyon soti la avan zéklè-a bwilé'w"* (*"*You damn fool, get the hell out of there before you are struck by the lightning"). The more the people persisted, the longer the Rastaman posed for Jah to take his photograph until one daring soldier in the crowd reached out and dragged him away, much against his will.

Meanwhile, the skies grew darker and darker by the second. The more the clouds advanced, the louder were the peals of thunder. The clouds hung heavily over the village like the stomach of a pregnant woman overlapping her trousers. The cloud had the tenacity of a pregnant woman on the verge of delivery. It would not deliver, despite its weight and pain. It stubbornly held back until the appointed moment came. Then it rained in torrents. "The gods, the people admitted, "they are angry. The lightning, the thunder and rain are signs of their disgust." In all of this, quite apart from reaching out to the bereaved families, and offering both families his condolences, Fr. Laport never uttered a word. His head was heavier than his heart. He had seen and heard too much for such a short time in the priesthood. Besides, it was his belief: "Play with the devil and he will come back to bite you." He wanted a way out of Bay-of-Ray. By then, the waters had risen to his chest. Fr. Laport felt that he was unable to swim with the tide. He needed some breathing space to reflect, to pray and to refocus. At that time, he felt he needed to find his center and his center was Christ. Like Peter, he had accepted the Lord's invitation to join him on the water, but for a minute, he had removed his eyes from the Lord and he was sinking. The daily travel between Potsville and Bay-of-Ray had taken its toll on Fr. Laport.

Obviously, the journey between Potsville and Bay-of-Ray grew more and more tedious. Fr. Laport meanwhile felt more and more as if his ministry was becoming monotonous. This was his first time as an acting Pastor. Thus, he thought it wise to consult with the Archbishop and discuss the possibility of releasing him of the charge of one of the parishes. In his mind, Fr. Laport thought it would be a lot better if he could settle down in one of the two parishes where he would be better able to carve out a pastoral vision and give some shape to his ministry. He did as he had planned and his consultation and suggestion with the Archbishop went very well. The option to choose a parish of his liking was thrown into his lap. He chose Potsville. Was Fr. Laport running from the pot into the fire? Would he, in Potsville, be exempted from the experiences he had had in his previous parishes? Only time would tell.

Chapter Six

Potsville

Potsville was the remotest and most quaint little village community on the West coast of Helen Island. For many years it was accessible only by sea. The descendants of French Creoles still inhabit Potsville. When sugar was king in Helen's kingdom, Potsville was the home of many sugar plantations. Potsville adopted many Black Africans, initially as slaves and later as freed coloured people.

Potsville had a population of about two thousand, most of whom were at the two extremes of the age bracket: the elderly and the very young. The age group in between was conspicuously absent. Why? Those who had the means migrated to London or other countries. They went in search of employment and a better livelihood. The few, who were left behind to care for the elderly, depended heavily on remittances. Others, to supplement the remittances, took employment in Félicitéville, or hired themselves as seasonal workers in neighbouring Martinique, Canada or the United Sates.

Potsville's job market was limited. It catered for the teaching profession, a village clerk, a librarian, farmers, fishermen and some sanitation workers. Policemen, nurses, and a medical professional were assigned from Félicitéville or elsewhere. Even the inhabitants themselves considered Potsville the little Siberia of Helen Island. Dissidents and underachievers were readily assigned to Potsville as a place for corrective measures. In their minds, too, any priest who resided among them had to be a "Mac-Gyver".

Potsville had its pros and cons. There were moments when Fr. Laport had some rather rude awakenings but there were times when he was treated as royalty there. Like Solfatara Town, Félicitéville,

Geckoville and Bay-of-Ray, Potsville had its own unique character and traditions and as many challenges. There were, of course, similarities and differences with the other communities of Helen Island. A large segment of the population in Potsville bore the features of the white European settlers. Their surnames were distinctly French. On the other hand, they also bore some similar features to the Caribs who were early settlers on various coastal sections of Helen Island. However, the larger segment of the population was of African descent. The African culture, though latent in the consciousness of African people in the Diaspora, was ever-present in their belief systems and, in particular, their belief in the spirit world. Some of these African traditions coexisted with their Catholicism as if there were no contradictions between the two. Potsville has its own history. The vestiges of the African culture were the most dominant of all and there was no shortage of stories concerning communion with the spirit world. Evil played a vital role in their consciousness too.

Maison Potsville was built by a very rich man. The villagers viewed him with deep suspicion. There was something stealthy about this gentleman. The source of his wealth and riches was the villagers' subject of debate but their social status placed them at a disadvantage. As slaves and servants, they could not openly challenge their master's authority. Conspiracy was rife among the villagers. They were determined to dig deep into their suspicions. As the master left late one night for his routine nocturnal rendezvous, the servants and field slaves conspired to keep watch. The wait was longer than expected. Some fell asleep. The night was dark. Under the cover of darkness one of the male slaves wandered into the village to visit a mistress. Just as he was stepping out of the mistress's home, about two o' clock in the morning, a huge bird with a large sack on its back flew overhead. The bird had just flown in from across the sea. Intimidated by this unusual sight, he screamed. His scream startled the bird. Its cargo fell to the ground. The scream alerted the sleeping villagers.

Soon everyone gathered to hear the story of what had happened. The poor slave, fearful for his life, was able to tell his story without naming the culprit. However, the man quickly retrieved the bag and opened it. It contained large sums of French currency. This poor man had divulged too much information to the villagers. It meant putting the master's reputation at risk. He was killed. His death was enough to intimidate the rest of his master's household and the villagers as well.

One night, Fr. Laport was awakened by an unusual flapping of wings. His curiosity too awoke from sleep with him. As he opened his bedroom window, right before his eyes, was quite a large bird. He had never, ever seen any bird of this magnitude before. It reminded him of an aircraft, but no aircraft would flap its wings like that. No aircraft would fly at such a low altitude between two buildings and at such low velocity. Fr. Laport's eyes followed the creature and noted where it came to rest. He recognized the house where the bird had landed. His night was sleepless. He kept a solitary vigil on his verandah. He was the village sentinel for the night.

There was a prayer meeting the following night and Fr. Laport found it expedient to mention the event. He did not have a clue as to who the individual was. All he said was that he had seen the house where the creature landed. A middle-aged woman was oblivious to her surroundings where lips were sealed and everyone was all ears. She knew nothing of the saying: "Discordant grumblings are no secrets." (Wis.1:11) Beneath her breath she misguidedly mumbled: *"Bondyé!Mi Fadda wè mwen!"* ("O my God! Father saw me!"). Parishioners who were to her immediate left and right in the pew, quickly turned in her direction, sized her up and down and in turn whispered to the next person what they had heard. Before long the pew was cleared. The middle aged woman was granted the isolation she begged for. She was left to face her embarrassment all on her own. While no one tortured her, nor was she burnt alive at the stake, she was left alone to bear the taunts of her own conscience. That conscience soon became Fr. Laport's nightmare. She placed it at his door.

For months, this poor woman daily and dutifully took up her position outside of Fr. Laport's presbytery from morning until night. Whenever Fr. Laport stepped out of his house, she stared at him from head to toe, hoping that he would be moved to say something to her but he never did. Veritably, her looks were the nonverbal plea of a mendicant desperate for recognition; one who was desperate for assistance but was just too ashamed to verbalize her needs lest she be showered with aspersions that would further trample on her already fragile ego. In her case there was no ego left. It was gone after her mumbled admission and a trampled ego. The story occupied a considerable length of time on Potsville's gossip circuit until Harrison's drama unfolded and blew it off the charts.

Harrison

Harrison was from Solfatara Town. His was the biggest and the longest story ever told since it was not something narrated or reported secondhand but something witnessed firsthand by all in Potsville one particular morning.

Fr. Laport received a telephone call from Solfatara Town very late one night. A woman's voice was heard on the other end of the line:

"Father, can you come to Solfatara Town immediately?"

"Woman, do you know what time of night it is?" he responded.

"No!" the woman replied.

"Well it's almost midnight. Please tell me, what's the matter?" asked Fr. Laport.

The woman responded,

"Father it's my helper. He looks like a real creature and is behaving like an animal."

"My dear," said Fr. Laport,

"Why don't you pray with him and I will see him in the morning?"
The woman intercepted, "It's urgent, Father, very urgent. Every time
I pray with him, he screams like an animal. I am scared."

"In that case," said Father,

"Can I talk with him on the phone?"

She handed the phone to Harrison.

"Hello Fadda,"

a voiced mourned on the phone.

"Hello Harrison, how are you?"

"Fadda I don't know. Fadda pray for me."

The moment Fr. Laport started praying with him, Harrison
roared at the top of his voice almost at the expense of Fr. Laport's
eardrum: "The phone is hot. It's burning my ears. I can't take it."
Acting on the advice of Fr. Laport, Harrison gave the phone back
to the woman; Father Laport advised her that Harrison should see
him the next morning. Sadly enough, he did not tell her what time
in the morning. At the back of his mind, he looked forward to seeing
Harrison at or about nine o'clock, the next day. He was not to be
so lucky. By six forty-five that morning, Harrison was already at
Father's door. The sight of Harrison sent shock waves through Fr.
Laport's entire body. For a quick moment, Fr. Laport was not sure
if he was a victim of instant epilepsy or if he was experiencing
delirious tremors or what exactly was assailing him. His limbs
became limp and his whole body went into convulsions. Regaining
some semblance of equilibrium, he stared Harrison in the face for
a second time. Before him stood a transfigured being that was no
longer human, but had only some human characteristics. The limbs
of his body were human but not his features. Faith and fate were
now having a tussle. Fr. Laport had to be strong - for himself and
for Harrison as well. Mustering some courage, Fr. Laport wiped his
face and gently asked Harrison to proceed to the church a few yards

away from the Presbytery and wait there for a while. He would join him shortly.

Fr. Laport sat down for a few minutes. To the best of his ability, he tried to normalize his racing heartbeat. It must have been racing at the pace of two hundred miles an hour. His trembling limbs and seized nerves had to be nursed back to normalcy before going to the church to attend to Harrison. The few minutes felt like a few years. The anxiety crept in and he feared that Harrison would think that Fr. Laport had taken him for granted. That was certainly not the issue at stake here. The real issue was that Fr. Laport was unprepared to handle a situation like this so early in the morning. Even worse, he was new to Potsville and he knew nobody who could assist him with an exorcism. He was left with few options but to confront the situation alone. He had to see Harrison. Fr. Laport finally left the presbytery and proceeded to the church. The one thought he carried with him as he walked to the church was, "I am not going to attempt an exorcism today!" All he wanted to do was to counsel Harrison as much as he could and to defer the exorcism for a later date. Thoughts and convictions formulated in the midst of fear are deceptive. Reality is reality. Fate and faith are seldom the same.

Fr. Laport arrived at the church and found Harrison's head buried in his lap. With extreme caution, he approached Harrison and directed him to walk with him in the direction of the Blessed Sacrament. Fr. Laport chose to sit with him before the Blessed Sacrament, knowing this to be the safest and most peaceful place in the church. As they sat in the presence of the Blessed Sacrament, Fr. Laport tried praying with Harrison. He asked him to repeat line by line and sometimes word by word. It was a simple prayer to the Holy Spirit asking God for guidance during the counselling session.

Oh Boy! Little did Fr. Laport know that he was about to open a Pandora's Box. Unannounced, Harrison transformed from a human to a lion. His face became that of a roaring lion. His eyes glittered like mirrors. His mouth swung open, his teeth were like fangs, and his throat was like a canyon. In one glance Fr. Laport looked down inside of Harrison's stomach. Oh boy! A new leash of energy surged through Fr. Laport's limbs and catapulted him to the nearest entrance of the church. Meanwhile, Harrison fitted himself under a stack of pews joined one to another, weighing well over four hundred pounds, and rattled them as if he was only shaking a twig.

The sound of the rattling pews echoed throughout the length and breadth of Potsville. In a matter of seconds, the whole village had crowded the church doors. The school bell was ignored and both teachers and children came rushing to the church to see firsthand what was happening. Fr. Laport's mind was in a virtual quandary. He was afraid for the safety of the school children and also for the safety of other vulnerable persons in the crowd. His primary concern then was to disperse the stubborn crowd that was anxious to witness an exorcism. A group of bulky men volunteered to restrain Harrison. Fr. Laport's approval was quickly given and he asked them to take Harrison into the sacristy for privacy reasons and to protect Harrison's identity as well.

Just then the police arrived and did a fantastic job at controlling the crowd. They ordered them back to the school. With the children out of the way, the police were able to bring the rest of the crowd under control. Then Fr. Laport ordered all doors of the church to be closed. A few elderly women, well known for conducting their private devotions after morning Mass, volunteered to assist as a backup prayer team. However Fr. Laport was still reluctant to proceed with an exorcism. Harrison kept manifesting and transforming. He threw himself headlong in every direction. He threw off the men who tried to restrain him as if they were mere pebbles. By then, Father was pink in the face and his eyes shifted from side to side as if searching for a way out of this. His legs were visibly wobbly. Thoughts of his frailty and mortality were visibly written all over his face. Yet Fr. Laport prayed earnestly. He begged God to bring them safely through it all and to speedily deliver Harrison, bringing this thing to an end. The test was getting more difficult case by case. Each exorcism was proving more difficult than the last. Fr. Laport paused and rested his thoughts for a while. Then a voice came from deep within: "I have made you little less than a god, crowned you with glory and honour. I have given you authority over the works of my hands, and put all things at your feet. (Ps.8:5)." Fr. Laport recognized that, just like the Psalmist David, the Lord was saying to him, "Put the thoughts of your human frailty and mortality at your back. Trust in the One who has called you and sent you." Fr. Laport had no intention of being another Jonah. He was not willing to spend even one hour, far less than a day or two, in the stomach of a whale. He would obey the Lord's command. He wanted the turbulent waters to recede. God was his only help in this matter.

Entering the sacristy, he armed himself with a purple stole, a crucifix, a vial of holy water, a jar of blessed salt and the prayer of exorcism. He was ready for battle. This time Fr. Laport had met his match. It was the mother of all battles. Harrison was restless. He had the strength of ten lions. Each time he opened his mouth it was like a deep canyon. Every word of prayer sent him berserk. He screamed and wiggled like a worm each time he was sprinkled with holy water. The holy water he claimed was like burning flames against his skin. As a last straw to that bitter cup, when Harrison opened his mouth one final time, Fr. Laport, threw into it a handful of blessed salt from his standing position. Something like a stream of smoke issued out of his mouth followed by a river of dark green bile. The men who tried to restrain him ran for cover, holding their noses and covering their mouths. The stench was awful. The bile was followed by another stream of smoke. Fr. Laport prayed and commanded whatever it was to leave Harrison and go to Jesus and be submissive to the voice of God. Finally Harrison fell to the floor like a ton of bricks and went to sleep. He slept soundly for a while. When he awoke from sleep, he was the weakest and the humblest gentleman imaginable.

A follow-up counselling session revealed a great deal: Harrison had in his possession a number of forbidden books and in reading them he had initiated himself into a cult which promised him a better and brighter future. Instead, he reaped a harvest of hell and damnation. What man would do to himself for the benefit of riches was indeed mind-boggling.

Poor Fr. Laport now had a new title bestowed upon him by the villagers of Potsville. Anticipating the worst, if this title were to go beyond Potsville he begged his parishioners to please spare him the embarrassment and to give God the glory. By then Bay-of-Ray and Potsville had sucked every bit of energy from Fr. Laport. He was staggering for want of physical as well as spiritual strength. He needed to be away from it all. A rest was not a luxury anymore but a necessity. Soon he boarded a flight and headed to the Virgin Islands to be with family and friends for a while. Later Fr. Laport commented, "God has a beautiful sense of humour." God himself, sometimes kicks up a storm to spur his prophets and priests into action, even when they least expect it.

God did not let Jonah rest while his people were in need of redemption. When Jonah fell asleep under the castor oil plant, God burnt it so that Jonah had to wake up and continue his journey to fulfill his mission. When Jonah was too weak for the journey, God provided him with bread and water. Even when Jonah, chose to go in the opposite direction to the one directed by God, a whale was lurking in the turbulent waters to take him to the destination God had in mind for him. Was that really the case with Fr. Laport's exhaustion and his need for rest?

Virgin Islands

While in the Virgin Islands, Fr. Laport substituted for the pastor of a particular parish there. He was all alone in the Presbytery. All doors were locked. Night had swooped in quickly. Worn out by the heat of the Virgin Islands sun, Fr. Laport decided to turn in as early as possible. He settled down in prayer. Suddenly, there was a stampede around him. It sounded like the ritual dance of some ancient African tribal religion. At once he thought to himself, "My imagination must be running amuck. My nerves must be giving way.' But no, they weren't. In tandem with the stampede, he heard voices jeering all around him. His body grew cold. Goose bumps draped his body like a cloak. His hair stood on end. Without a word, Fr. Laport got to his feet, grabbed a bottle of holy water and some blessed salt. He blessed the room and then the entire Presbytery. All was silent again.

The next morning he was locked out of his private bathroom. 'What on earth is happening in this place?' he asked. "Did I skip ship from Helen's shores only to fall into deeper turbulent waters?" Fr. Laport knew there was no one present in the flesh and he never expected a verbal response. If perchance he had received a verbal response no speedometer or pedometer could have accurately measured the rate of his flight. Fr. Laport turned his attention to St. Michael the Archangel, the defender of God's people in battle. As he invoked St. Michael, the door opened. No one was seen leaving the bathroom. It was then that it dawned on Fr. Laport that the name which he received at Confirmation was Michael. "My God!" he bellowed. "I hope you did not give me this name other than to have Michael as one of my patron saints and my guardian angel." Who knows? God has strange ways of doing what he will. After all, that's why he is God, and man is his image on earth (Ps.8).

Later that morning, Fr. Laport set out for the Post Office. On entering a blue 1980 Chevrolet hatchback provided for his use, he placed the key in the ignition and started the car. Without warning, the air-conditioning system switched on of its own accord and blasted his face with dust and dried leaves. This he thought was some malfunction on the part of the car. He readily dismissed it from his mind and continued on his way to the Post Office. On returning to the car after completing all his transactions, he got in the car and the same thing happened again. This time, Fr. Laport was convinced that the car needed to be sent to the dealers for repairs lest somebody got injured. What Fr. Laport did not know, since he was no fortuneteller, was that something big awaited him on his return to the Presbytery.

As he stepped through the door of the Presbytery, he was intercepted by a young man who asked, "Are you the priest?" "Yes, I am," replied Fr. Laport, "What can I do for you?" The young man replied, "I want to kill myself." Thinking that it was all a joke and that the young man simply intended to try his patience, Fr. Laport replied, "Would you like me to get you a length of rope?" At these words, the eyes of the young man fell to the ground. Then Fr. Laport said to him, 'Follow me'. Unknowingly, once again, Fr. Laport had bitten the tip of a poisoned arrow. What he thought would have been only a counselling session was once more a dive into the spirit world.

The youth was adamant: he wanted to kill himself. All he knew was that the time had come and he must die. As he spoke, Fr. Laport paid close attention to his demeanor. There was something unusual about it. He spoke of the attempts he had made on his life prior to coming to the Presbytery to seek help. Then he admitted that it was one of his friends who had invited him to kill himself in a fake car crash the day before.

"Where is your friend?" asked Fr. Laport.

"Me eh know," he replied in his native Virgin Islander accent.

"Does he have a name and telephone number that you would like to share with me?" He answered, "Yea."

Then he gave Fr. Laport both the name and number willingly. At which point Father also thought it necessary to ask for his parents' names, address and telephone number as well. It was a good thought. With the youth's permission, Fr. Laport contacted the friend and had a brief conversation with him, without divulging any information.

"Hi! This is Fr. Laport. How are you doing today?"

In his true Virgin Islander accent the young man answered "Me doing good man."

"I'm calling with regards to your friend, Amigo. When last did you see him?"

"Me nah see da man, lang lang time you know."

By the tone of the young man's responses, Fr. Laport reckoned that something was amiss. He decided there and then to redirect the course of the conversation between himself and Amigo, this time concentrating on his family history and his ancestors as far back as he was able to recall. Amigo did not have to look very far back into his ancestry. His grandfather was the culprit. As soon as the conversation turned in the direction of his grandfather, Amigo grew excessively restless. As soon as Fr. Laport asked him the name of his grandpa, Amigo's eyes popped right out of their sockets, his tongue thickened in his mouth, and his body ejected out of the chair like a parachute. Amigo slammed himself against the wall in the office. Then he came crashing to the floor like a ton of bricks.

Maria, a high school girl while on vacation, was serving as an interim receptionist. She heard the commotion followed by the crash and quickly entered the office to find out if Fr. Laport needed any assistance. When Maria saw the young man lying helplessly on the floor, she froze for a while. Meanwhile, Fr. Laport sat quietly at the desk with his index finger pasted across his lips. He was numb. Not a thought crossed his mind at that moment. It was only when Maria screamed out, "Father, are you okay?" that Fr. Laport reacted and turned in Maria's direction. Once again, Fr. Laport felt that God had seduced him and duped him. What help, he thought, could Maria have offered him? Not much. Hesitantly he asked her,

"Can you sit at your desk and pray the Rosary for me and Amigo?"
"Of course, Father, I'll be more than happy to do so."

Father made no attempt to disturb Amigo from his sleep. Instead, he took the opportunity to call his family to the office. Their response was prompt. In a matter of minutes the family was at the door. The receptionist ushered them into the office where they joined Amigo, who was still dazed. Fr. Laport recounted what had transpired earlier. Then the family volunteered the needed information about the grandfather, who was allegedly a terror in his youth, and one who had left a trail of victims in his path.

The grandpa had committed suicide by jumping off a multi-storey building many years earlier. The family then asked what could be done to remedy the situation. Walking the family through the process, Fr. Laport instructed them to invoke the spirit of their grandpa and commend his soul to the Lord. He recommended that Requiem Masses, be celebrated for the repose of his soul. The family then suggested that in the process, a Mass should be celebrated for the healing of their family tree during which they would join in praying for the redemption of their grandpa's soul. Father agreed. Amigo's immediate family members were very devout Catholics.

A few days later, after much intense preparation with those concerned, family and friends gathered at home for the Mass. All was calm until grandpa's name was being invoked at the general intercession and his soul was commended to the Lord. Grandpa was definitely bent on creating havoc before his departure. Tumult ensued everywhere: inside as well as outside of the home. Doors and windows independently opened and closed. They banged, they slammed, and curtains flew in all directions. Every telephone in the home rang consistently. The dogs on the outside were hysterical and so were all the other animals in the yard.

Everyone was tense. Fr. Laport urged everyone to persist in prayer and not to allow themselves to be distracted by the din and confusion for it was all a willful diversion to deter the prayers and to delay the soul's departure. The distraction ensued for well over half an hour, after which all went silent again. By then, everyone in attendance was drenched in sweat. Amigo, meanwhile, sat still in the distant, wondering what had happened. His mother approached him and asked him if he was okay. He came to his senses and asked, "What was grandpa doing here? And why was he creating such hell before walking out of the house in such a rage?" Fr. Laport took the opportunity at the end of the Mass to remind Amigo's family to continue praying for the repose of grandpa's soul.

Fr. Laport meanwhile was thinking that his crusade against evil spirits in the Virgin Islands had ended but Maria, the part time receptionist, had another assignment lined up for him. After witnessing all that had happened at the Presbytery, she must have reported the whole affair to her parents. Her family seemed to have been victims of a similar fate to Amigo's family. The next thing Fr. Laport knew was that an appointment had been arranged for him to meet with Maria's family. He was left totally in the dark as to the nature of the meeting. Learning of the appointment, Fr. Laport mumbled under his breath, "But this is hardly a vacation. I came here to rest." His spirit was protesting! His conscience lashed back without warning, "Didn't you try extending your vacation the last time you visited London, England?" Wow! What a rude reminder! Memory may be latent but conscience never sleeps. The prophet's words came home to him: "Can a man cheat God?" The answer to the prophet's question is, "No!" And it is more unconscionable for a priest to attempt to cheat God. Fr. Laport's conscience was under heavy attack. "How can you tell God you are on vacation?" his conscience asked. Immediately the words of Wisdom were ringing in his ears:

"If as administrators of his kingdom, you have not
governed justly, nor observed the law, nor behaved as
God would have you behave, he will fall on you swiftly
and terribly. Ruthless judgement is reserved for the high
and mighty; the lowly will be compassionately pardoned,
the mighty will be mightily punished (Wis.6:4-7)."

Almost like a dog, Fr. Laport barked "Wow, wow, wow." He
paused for a while. Then he mumbled to himself, "Don't mess with
God. God is a double-edged sword." For God's words can slit through
bone and marrow. He certainly knows how and when to provoke the
cognizance of the conscience and to humble the haughty for their
own good and salvation.

Without further ado, Fr. Laport agreed to meet with Maria's
family. He listened to their story and soon realized that they too
needed as much help as Amigo's family. Grandpa was a member
of a secret society and he had died an inhumane, ignominious and
mysterious death. Since his death Maria's family had been disturbed
by some strange presence in the home. A shadow always followed
members of the family around. Although the family had migrated
from Trinity Islands to the Virgin Islands, the shadow still haunted
them. Sometimes the shadow appeared to show signs of frustration
and disgust, and whenever it did, the entire family was set in uproar.
It was all a mystery to them. Yet they appeared to be the most loving
and united family.

Fr. Laport agreed to assist the family. A house Mass was
scheduled at the home of the family two days later at ten o'clock in
the morning. On entering the home, Fr. Laport was brushed by a
gale of wind. Maria's father, who met Fr. Laport at the door, asked
him, "Did you see what walked across the door as you entered?"
"No," answered Fr. Laport, "all I felt was a gush of wind." "Oh"
replied Maria's father. They both ended the conversation at that

point. Before the commencement of the Mass, Fr. Laport explained at length to the family what was about to happen. The atmosphere was tense but the family sang and prayed. They were devout Catholics. At the intercessory prayers, Grandpa was addressed by name. He was commanded to come to Jesus by first forgiving those who had subjected him to the inhumane, ignominious and mysterious death. Goose bumps were growing on everyone's skin like mushrooms. Three times this prayer was repeated. On the third occasion the door opened of its own accord and something like a gale of wind was sucked out of the door, slamming it shut. The family sat transfixed in their seats. The last disturbance came during the Eucharistic prayer when Grandpa's name was mentioned. Fr. Laport spoke the words:

> "Remember your servant N, whom you have called (Today) from this world to yourself. Grant that he (she) who was united with your Son in a death like His, may also be one with Him in His Resurrection."[1]

A gentle breeze blew through the room. The air was tranquil and warm. A very peaceful atmosphere enveloped the room for the duration of Mass; Maria's father noted that it was at that point in the Mass, for the first time since his father's death, that he had felt a sense of detachment from his father. The good news was, according to Maria's father, who later recounted, that their home and lives were left in peace since that day. It was not only their home that enjoyed an atmosphere of peace. Fr. Laport too was left in peace until his return to Potsville. What a welcome breath of fresh air it was for him to enjoy a season free from chasing spirits and demons. How long would that lull last? It lasted until Fr. Laport was transferred to Cane City.

---

[1] Masses for the Dead, Eucharist Prayer II, Cf. The Roman Missal, English Translation According to the Third Typical Edition, Catholic Truth Society, St. Paul Publications 2010, p.682

Chapter Seven

Cane City

In the early days of the crystal king, immigrants from all parts of Helen Island gave birth to and shaped the identity of Cane City. It was really a hodgepodge of Afro, Anglo, Franco and Indo cultures. The Afro-Franco culture was the dominant culture there. It was a culture born and carved out of a struggle. It was born in a spirit of resistance and emerged as the identity of an oppressed people. A people born in slavery were destined for continuous servitude. However, their determination and resilience made their efforts for freedom more demanding. Freedom is a precious commodity for those who are willfully deprived of it. People oppressed in every sense of the word: physically, emotionally, economically, socially and spiritually, understood that there was a way out of this malaise and they were willing to shed their own blood, and even to sell their own souls in exchange for freedom. Fr. Laport observed that where true Christian spirituality and values were lacking, the adversary of faith raised its ugly head and the people pursued freedom at any cost. Their souls were the currency spent in the process which only perpetuated the same cycle of human desecration from which they longed to be free.

Fr. Laport considered the people of Cane City as desecrated humans. They were victims of cracking whips. The souls of their ancestors were in a perpetual state of lamentation. These souls begged for a requiem which could not be paid for in the currency earned with the sweat of their children. The same indomitable spirit which characterized their children and their children's children through many generations was the spirit which often found expression in their practice of cults within Catholicism. The two were so closely knit that they did not see any disparity between them.

It was this practice of Afro-traditions within Catholicism that had often been the cause of their condemnation as a superstitious people. In communities where vestiges of African traditional religious expressions lingered, people unfamiliar with them, narrowly perceived them as devil worship. Such accusation and stigma were sometimes unfair. While the African traditional religion remained an underground religion throughout its existence, what had survived and was more openly practised were witchcraft, black magic and necromancy. None of these were part of traditional African religion. *Kèlé* was the lone African traditional religion to survive the onslaught of European bias and bigotry in Helen Island. Fr. Laport's battle so far had been a battle against witchcraft, black magic and necromancy which seemed to haunt him wherever he went.

Each parish, city, town and village community thus far had been for Fr. Laport an 'open university' and a 'seminary'. Cane City was no exception in this regard.

When Fr. Laport arrived in Cane City, he was bewildered by the condition of the physical structures that he inherited. The presbytery was simply a termite's heaven. The church building stood like an old book breaking loose at the seams. The furniture was like the ragged book pages, worn out by frequent use and age. The Parish Hall was best described as a bat and rat sanctuary. He knew there was work to be done. However, the income was so thin that he wondered what sustained his predecessors. He concluded that the poor priests must have been handicapped by the lack of income and could not afford to leave behind anything better. Believing in Divine providence, he still undertook the risk of restoring the presbytery. With the assistance of his Archbishop, he secured a loan and successfully completed the renovations.

However, it was more than the physical structures which needed urgent attention. The human and spiritual structures needed just as much attention. Adopting the same methods as he did in Solfatara Town and Potsville, he soon set himself the task of a community by community evangelization outreach program. By the end of the Lenten season, Cane City Parish was on fire and the monetary collection had increased three hundred fold. This amount was still insufficient to undertake any renovation work on the church building itself. In April of that year, Fr. Laport suffered a heart attack while preaching at an evangelization mission. Soon rumors went around Cane City that Fr. Laport was the victim of an evil attack. Ma Pépé was to be held fully responsible for Fr. Laport's condition. From where did this rumour emanate? To this day it's still a mystery. All Fr. Laport remembered by way of contact with Ma Pépé was that a few days after his arrival, he had had a dream of a woman coming to his office. The woman was wearing a plaid dress, a large straw hat, and carrying a brown side bag over her left shoulder and she wore brown shoes. The dream was meaningless at the time. Much to his surprise, while seated in his office preparing for an evening service, lo and behold this woman walked in unannounced on the last stroke of the Angelus. She stood in the exact spot, as in the dream and was dressed exactly as she had appeared before him in the dream. Goose bumps grew on every part of Fr. Laport's body. His blood ran cold. He was even speechless for a while. Standing with her left hand akimbo and her eyes riveted to the wall before her, she introduced herself as Ma Pépé, the mother of the parish and Father was free to consult her before any action could be undertaken in Cane City.

"Wow! Wow! Wow!" Fr. Laport repeated, "You are the mother of the parish eh?" Ignoring her impertinence, Fr. Laport interrupted her conversation: "Ma Pépé, time is against us. Shall we proceed to church and we'll continue this conversation at a more convenient time?" While Father Laport never uttered a word to anyone, the dream took on a new meaning that night. Her demeanour too left Fr. Laport with a lot of food for thought but only time would reveal the connection between the rumour, the dream and Ma Pépé's imprudent remarks.

At Sunday morning Mass, at the intercessions, Ma Pépé was seen striding toward the sanctuary. Father asked one of the senior altar servers: "Who is this woman?" "Ma Pépé," was his reply. "Where is she going?" "Father," the altar server responded, "It's her habit. Every Sunday she comes up to the lectern to chastise the congregation." "What?" Father asked; "Please ask her to take her seat." At this point her facial expression was not befitting the expression of a Christian. After the post Communion Prayer, again Ma Pépé was seen moving in the direction of the lectern. Father immediately asked the same senior altar server to ask Ma Pépé to take her seat and not repeat her performance. Again, her actions were unbecoming for a person in church and one who had just moments before received the Holy Eucharist.

During the weekly notices Fr. Laport made the following announcements:

- Persons with prayer intentions please bring them to the Parish Office on Thursday afternoons by three o'clock.
- Persons with parish related notices should do the same by Thursday no later than three o' clock in the afternoon each week.

By the time the final blessing was given, Ma Pépé had taken her position at the main entrance. Fr. Laport was hardly out of the door when she accosted him. She told him in no uncertain terms "I am the mother of the parish. Every Sunday I must do my own prayers and notices. Nobody can explain my notices as I do." "In that case Ma Pépé," Father replied, "Write your intentions and notices just the way you deliver them every Sunday and I will insert them in their appropriate place." Her candid response was, "Unless I do it myself, it will not be done." "Okay Ma Pépé, have it your way, but the liturgy will not be used for personal mileage." She galloped away with the meanest look on her face.

On Tuesday morning, news reached Fr. Laport that Ma Pépé had been soliciting the help of the bus drivers in the community to organize a demonstration at the Archbishop's office to get Fr. Laport out of Cane City. The bus drivers were not prepared to get involved. Instead, each bus driver she approached took the opportunity to chastise her for her obnoxious behaviour on the altar year in and year out. Moreover, people were celebrating the fact that she had been stopped by Fr. Laport. Anger masked her face every time she crossed the path of Fr. Laport. He paid her no mind; on the contrary, he greeted her with utmost respect and treated her as he would any parishioner in Cane City.

The time came to renovate the church building. Consultants recommended that it be demolished. The structure was too weak to sustain any form of renovation or restoration. Therefore, it would be an utter waste of good money to renovate. Ma Pépé was back in circulation again and this time she was prepared to do all within her power to stall that project. Plans for the project dragged on for more than two years. During that time Ma Pépé was in her element. Her efforts were gaining momentum. A group of similar minded old women joined her cause. They bitterly contested the need for a new church building. Meanwhile donations kept pouring in and parishioners were becoming overtly generous, much to the anger of Ma Pépé and her group of protesters. There is a saying in Helen Island; "The devil will not prevent the funeral from taking place." At the appointed time, all approvals were met and the contractor was given the all-clear to demolish the building. The process was earmarked to take a week but owing to the fragile nature of the structure, it was crumbled in one hour. Ma Pépé's anger had only just started blazing. Parishioners still questioned her motives. Something, somewhere was amiss. Would patience and time reveal the true nature of the beast?

The time came for the excavation of the sanctuary. Ma Pépé's temper was on the verge of explosion. Almost in military style, she and her cohort marched around the ruins as if they were soldiers on parade, condemning Fr. Laport for the desecration of what they called their sacred shrine. The original podiums were pulled down and then the huge concrete altar that was anchored into the ground by lengths of steel. During the excavation, directly beneath the altar, three bottles were recovered containing parchment paper with strange inscriptions written on them. One of the workers immediately raised an alarm, "What on earth are these things doing under the altar?" With one glance, Ma Pépé recognized the bottles. She went livid. Her voice went silent. Whatever she must have said to her cohort, they too followed suit. Within seconds they were gone like the wind. From that day onward the open protest ended. Why? Only time would tell.

Tell-A-Person Communication lines were overloaded within seconds. Parishioners gathered to see the exhibits for themselves. Suspicion was rife. All fingers were now pointed in the direction of Ma Pépé who by then had earned the reputation of a witch. People believed that at long last her power and her stronghold over the parish had come to an end. If the discovery was a setback for her, it certainly did not mark the end of her efforts to deter the progress of the project. Her bag of antics was never empty.

This time Ma Pépé was determined to eliminate Fr. Laport at any cost. Word went round that Fr. Laport would be leaving Helen for the United States for medical attention. Ma Pépé wasted no time. She had plans in place ready for execution. A member of her cohort, armed with a $100.00 note, stood watch at the entrance of the presbytery for the whole day. He waited for Fr. Laport whom he knew had an evening service in anticipation of an early departure next morning.

As soon as Father emerged, the adherent approached him. He greeted Fr. Laport in the most humble and genuine tone. His speech was mellow, yet it was a voice pregnant with malice. Fr. Laport smiled. Then the cohort took Fr. Laport's left hand into his right and pressed the hundred dollar note into it with these words, "My mother, Ma Pépé, has asked me to deliver this to you. She said, on your way to the airport tomorrow; go to Paul's drugstore, in Stone Town. She has spoken with the druggist there. He will give you a vial of medicine which you must take with you to the United States. She has advised me to tell you not to take it while on the flight but as soon as you arrive at your destination. Before you sleep pour it into a glass of water and drink all of it at once. You are sure to be cured of your heart condition."

Fr. Laport giggled at the stupidity of the adherent. His eyes were like shifting sand. Guilt was written all over his face. With a sharp scrutiny of his face, Fr. Laport read the word "Deception" carved on it. Pretending as if he were totally ignorant of what was happening, Fr. Laport kindly returned her courtesy with thanks and insisted that he would stop and, pick up the medicine but would pay for it out of his own pocket. The devotee persisted with his offer. Fr. Laport then signaled the gardener to collect the money and dispose of it as he saw fit.

He had hardly arrived in the United Sates than word went round Cane City. Ma Pépé had it that when Fr. Laport left that morning, his health had deteriorated and his condition was not promising. She was asking parishioners to be on standby. She was absolutely sure to hear reports of Fr. Laport's death at any minute. Contrary to her wish, her $100.00 bill never left Cane City and Father's feet never touched the steps of Paul's drugstore. A guilty conscience has no secret chambers. Ma Pépé was duty bound to make a public confession.

The morning after Fr. Laport returned from the United States, the telephone rang. A newly appointed Assistant Priest to Fr. Laport was near the phone upstairs. Unknowingly, he and Fr. Laport picked up the phone together but his Assistant beat him to saying hello. Hearing Ma Pépé's voice at the end of the line, Fr. Laport decided to eavesdrop on the conversation. Unwittingly, she was about to divulge her murder plot.

"Where is your friend?" she asked the assistant. He answered, "I don't know hon!" To this Ma Pépé stated *"Mwen èk Poli manntjé'y pwèmyé fwa-a, lot kou-a nou pakay mantjé'y."* Meaning: "This time he had escaped the noose set by Poli and me; the next time he will not." Fr. Laport's jaw dropped like a ton of bricks. This was too much for his ears. He decided to eavesdrop on any subsequent calls that morning. It was hardly a minute later when the phone rang again. It was Ruffina from Yam Village just a few miles outside of the parish church. Her question and statement were identical to that of Ma Pépé.

From this moment, Fr. Laport knew he was treading on thin ice. To all of this, Father's assistant simply remarked: "You people are in love. I will stay clear of your love affair." The poor priest was clueless as to what was unfolding. To protect his innocence, he was left clueless.

Time was running out for Ma Pépé; the project was drawing to an end. She was desperate. It was a Sunday morning; Mass was coming to a close. At that time, Mass was held in an adjacent school building just a stone's throw from the church building under reconstruction. Oblivious of her surroundings, Ma Pépé blurted out, "I do not know why this priest would not just drop dead." The congregation went silent and much to her embarrassment, she was forced to walk away of her own accord.

In all of this, her pugnacious spirit would not rest. She was as determined as her master, the devil. She wanted Fr. Laport dead. The night was still young. It was about eight o'clock on a day that had not been hectic, yet Fr. Laport felt exhausted. Much as he tried to stay awake, it was just impossible. When he had exhausted all efforts to keep his eyes open, he landed himself face down on his bed. No sooner had he landed on his bed than a force grabbed hold of him at the back of his head and pressed hard as could be, forcing his mouth and nose as deep as possible into the pillow. Initially, Fr. Laport put up a struggle, then held his breath; he faked death. Believing he was really dead, a voice said *"Selèp sé pa jodi mewen té ja vlé twjé'w."* Meaning: 'You son of a gun, I've been longing to kill you for a long time.' The hand withdrew. Fr. Laport maintained his stillness a while and then gradually shifted his head to the side, only to see what looked like a four foot florescent tube moving out of his bedroom door. Pulling himself together, he prayed for God's protection. The rest of the night sleep evaded his eyes until daybreak.

The following Sunday, after the morning Mass, Fr. Laport briefed the congregation of the incident. No names were mentioned. No person was singled out in any way. Ma Pépé stood up and shouted over the heads of the congregation, "Tell you all priest do not mention my name."

Silence gripped the congregation. Had a pin fallen to the ground, people in Bay-of-Ray would have heard it. Almost desperate to achieve some form of damage control, Ma Pépé grabbed her brother by the arm and told him to demand an apology from Fr. Laport on her behalf. Her brother, without hesitation, retorted "Get me out of your mess. I was in church and never once did I hear the priest call your name. If you are guilty, then let your guilt be upon your head." "You are a traitor!" she shouted. Hum! Cane City was abuzz. As for Ma Pépé, nothing would change her.

Making Bread on the Dead

It was a weekday morning. Very few persons had attended Mass that day. That particular morning, Fr. Laport had preached on the honesty and integrity of Christians in transacting business.

He warned that Christians in business must safeguard the interest and the health of customers and consumers in every way possible. He recalled how in his youth, rumour had it that certain bakers sometimes mingled the remains of dead people in their dough in an attempt to keep customers loyal to them. "This," Fr. Laport assured his congregation "should never happen among you." The words were hardly out of his mouth when Ma Pépé's head receded into her body like a turtle sheltering its head from an attack. For the remainder of the Mass, Ma Pépé's head never emerged from her body, nor did she receive Holy Communion that morning. At the final blessing, she was still glued to the pew.

As soon as Fr. Laport emerged from the sacristy, Ma Pépé sped off ahead him, desperate to keep out of his path. Fr. Laport walked slowly behind her. Suddenly, the gravedigger emerged from under the hill. As soon as she spotted him, she launched an attack on him. "Jamebo!" she shouted, "did I ever send you to get the skull of any dead person for me from the cemetery?" "But of course," Jamebo responded, "you paid me $40.00 when I gave you the skull. Remember, it was covered with maggots." "Jamebo!" Ma Pépé screamed, "I've warned you before. I've had reasons to take you to court for this sometime before." "Ma Pépé, I am not lying on you. Look de priest there listening to everything. Fadda give me absolution. I confess already, in public Fadda." Without further ado, not even turning back to see if Fr. Laport was there or not, Ma Pépé launched off like a rocket heading for space.

In the afternoon of that same day, Ma Pépé returned to confront Fr. Laport. Oh what a dreadful mistake on her part! It was Fr. Laport's opportunity to confront her once and for all. He put on a bold front. At the end of all her accusations he told her to her face, "You are the only creature I've seen with four faces and six tongues." Fr. Laport knew it was a very low blow. At the tone of his statement, she squirmed in her skin. She fumbled for words. For a woman so loquacious, she was bankrupt for words. She sauntered to her left and then to her right looking for a last means of defence, but none was forthcoming. Her ultimate effort failed when she tried to outstare Fr. Laport. She withdrew like white lightning. She must have remembered that the eyes are the mirror of the soul. Courage failed her this time; she walked away but Fr. Laport knew deep in his heart that that was not the end of her.

The next morning her brother from Félicitéville was brought in to plead her case and to justify her cause for beatification. Fr. Laport calmly directed him – just in case he did not know of her public confession in church – to consult with his brother in Yam Village. The subject ended there. Ma Pépé's nocturnal activities were the subject of much debate in Cane City. It appeared that she never slept. Her grandson publicly admitted, "Whenever granny is missing, the broom goes missing too." Another of her partners admitted to a novice witch, "Ma Pépé is the queen of the lot. Her flying skills are unsurpassable but she cannot fly too high because her breasts are too short."

The church rebuilding project had come to a successful completion. Preparations were in full swing for the dedication. Joiners were in a heated race with the clock. They were competing with time to complete and install new pews. The seating capacity was one thousand five hundred persons. Volunteers worked in tandem like pistons to prepare the church. In the wee hours of Sunday morning, the day of dedication, Ma Pépé showed up and started giving directions. With a patience worn thin over the years by Ma Pépé's controlling attitude, an elderly gentleman "went ballistic." He commanded her to extend her breast as she did the whole night long and to fly to the furthest ends of the earth. "You are the devil," he said, "who is always obstructing a religious procession."

By dawn Sunday morning, fresh rumors were circulating. The same senior altar server who had intercepted Ma Pépé on her way to the podium, was being accused of misconduct and calls were everywhere for his expulsion from his post as senior altar server. Fr. Laport, on another hand, was being accused of misappropriation of parish and building funds. Many treated the accusations merely as accusations and nothing more; the zeal of Ma Pépé and her cohort was flagging. Once this reached the Bishop's ears, the dedication ceremony, scheduled for four o'clock that Sunday afternoon, would have to be postponed, so she thought.

As it turned out, the ceremony proceeded without a hitch. The accusations all dissipated like thin smoke for lack of substance and veracity. Ma Pépé was left to languish and to wallow in her own mess for the rest of her life. Shortly thereafter, Fr. Laport, feeling that his ministry and usefulness in Cane City had reached its fruition, acceded gracefully to a transfer to Boloville and Rest Town in the south of Helen Island.

Ritual Murder in Félicitéville

While Fr. Laport was in the process of transitioning to Boloville and Rest Town, news was breaking of a ritual murder in Félicitéville. The news was gruesome. It was chilling to say the least. During his ministry, Fr. Laport had heard enough. His soul had endured its fair share of experiences so that he was resigned not to entertain anything more about the world of spirits and demons. He found deep consolation in the fact that this gruesome act was beyond the boundaries of his pastoral territory. The impact was no doubt emotionally daunting for the families, as well as for the nation. It was a challenge to the faith of the local Church for the misguided victims had beguiled themselves into thinking that human life was the cheapest commodity to be placed on the altar of wants and greed. People had become hard-hearted and were not concerned about the consequences of this type of uncivilized and dehumanized behaviour and its consequences on Helen's society – diminishing Christians' values and threatening family life and the stability of the community.

However, Fr. Laport was eager to forget the whole thing and let the guys in Félicitéville deal with the issue. He wanted no part of it and wished himself far away from Félicitéville and beyond the reach of everyone concerned. He did not know the party involved. That made the situation more impersonal and allowed him to distance himself with a measure of calm indifference.

God is God and will always be God. His ways are not our ways. He reads our thoughts from far away. He knows his reluctant prophets who are contented to do their mere duty and no more, and at the peril of losing their souls, adopt an indifferent attitude because of the dangers and hardship involved in helping people. He knows exactly the precise moment to permit the worm to attack the roots of the castor oil plant. He allows it to wither.

Fr. Laport had spoken too quickly. He had just ceased to reflect on the turbulent waters when the telephone rang. The call was from his longtime friends, Carinthia and Gavel. After relating the news to Father, they added, "And the sad part of it all, Father, is that the accused is Gavel's nephew, Julian." Fr. Laport was shocked and numbed, and he became rigid. He was speechless. "Hello, are you there?" they asked, "Ye, ye, yes, I am," murmured Fr. Laport, "I'm, I'm, I'm listening." Fr. Laport was at a loss for words as Carinthia and Gavel described the murder. As they continued their graphic description, Fr. Laport got more and more upset. At one point, he begged them to hold the line for a minute and headed straight to the washroom where he emptied the contents of his stomach. When Fr. Laport resumed the conversation, they asked, "Father, are you okay?" He concealed his pain, put on a bold front, cleared his throat and spruced up his voice, "Oh yea, I'm okay. I'm doing fine. Indeed I'm more concerned about you guys." Then what Father feared most was next on their agenda, "Father," Carinthia and Gavel asked in vulnerable tones, "Can you join the family in prayer?" Conscious of his calling, he dared not refuse them. His conscience would not permit him to.

A line in the Lord's Prayer streamed through his mind: "Forgive us our trespasses as we forgive those who trespass against us." "What's the connection?" he asked himself. Then Fr. Laport understood that the Lord was saying: "if you can't show compassion to the vulnerable in time of need, why should you expect mercy and compassion from me?" He chuckled and said, "Okay, God I'm not prepared to be the meal of any whale right now. I will do whatever you tell me. I will go wherever you send me."

The gruesomeness unfolded further when Father met with the family face to face. Julian, they admitted, had gone berserk. Why? They were clueless. It was a mystery to everyone. Julian was a brilliant scholar. For fear that speculation had misled them; Father implored the family to leave the diagnosis to the competency of the medical professionals. As they wept, they repeated the sequence of events over and over again. "Julian," they mourned, "attacked his uncle, bashed his head, ripped his eyes out of their sockets, and swallowed them." Their souls were linked in fraternity to Julian's soul. They anguished over him even though he was still numb as to what he had done. The family was still grateful that Julian had been restrained before he attempted to nibble at his uncle's brain. Sympathetic onlookers had crowded round and restrained him. Although Julian had had the strength of a legion, he was subdued, and the crowd held him and handed him over to the police when they arrived on the scene. By then his uncle was dead. The horror of it all was more than Fr. Laport's stomach could bear. Bile had climbed up his esophagus like a tsunami. In a matter of minutes, Father was mute. He had to resort to sign language when he needed directions to the restroom.

Fr. Laport prayed with the family and consoled them as best he could. Prior to his departure, he advised the family to seek the assistance of the priests in Félicitéville, since he was making final preparations to assume duties in Boloville and Rest Town. His advice fell on deaf ears. Their eyes focused directly into his and with the most pathetic look on their faces, they begged, "Father, please we beg you," they said, "do us a favour. Have a word with him and say a prayer with Julian for us." Fr. Laport at that moment, felt as if invisible maggots had crawled all over his body. Again his faith and compassion did not permit him to say "no", but left to nervousness alone, the "no" would have been loud and clear. Out of the blue, the Lord reminded him of his promise to do whatever He told him and go wherever He sent him.

Julian was under detention at the Green Mental Hospital. The nurse on duty was a close friend of Fr. Laport and she graciously permitted him to visit Julian. One of the orderlies on duty directed Fr. Laport to the cell where Julian was kept under watch night and day. The mere sight of the patient sent shockwaves through Father's spine. Fr. Laport felt his body drift from left to right, then forward and then backward. His legs were weak. With a drunkard's gait, he made his way alongside the orderly. He forced himself to conceal his fears as best he could and he succeeded. Julian sat on the bare concrete floor stark naked. His back was against an iron grill, his hands and feet restrained with white bands of cloth. His eyes were dazed and distant, his lips ajar and he dribbled over his tummy, Fr. Laport's mind was in revulsion and so was his stomach.

A chair was brought into Julian's detention cell for Fr. Laport. There, the two were left alone. No one knew what was rummaging through Father's mind at the time. Fatalism and faith were indeed in a deep tussle as long as the visit lasted. The silence between Fr. Laport and Julian was long and pregnant. What the visit was expected to achieve was anybody's guess. For a moment, Fr. Laport took a long hard look at Julian's stomach and wondered what the heck was happening to his uncle's eyes in there. His skin crawled. Goose bumps were like sleeves, the full length of his arms. As time went by, he mustered a little courage and asked Julian, 'How are you?' The young man answered as if in a drunken stupor, his tongue as heavy as bricks, 'I, I, I are there.' At least the ice was broken and a dialogue, although very tiring, ensued. For all his efforts to stimulate a conversation, Fr. Laport soon deduced that it was not the best day for Julian to be forced to talk. He prayed over Julian and made his exit. Father promised Julian that he would visit again, but did not say when.

A few days later, Julian was more coherent. It would be possible to hold a logical conversation with him. Fr. Laport was informed of his improvement. Without delay, Father visited him. The two had quite an animated conversation. Without a doubt, Julian was cognizant of what had happened. He was most remorseful but his conscience was merciless. He knew there was no way in which he could compensate for his deceased uncle. How would he face his family members? Would his family ever forgive him? Could he ever be truthful with them and tell them what led him to such a gruesome act? He was in a really deep quandary.

He'd brought himself to the point where Fr. Laport wanted him to be, and so Father profited the opportunity to ask, "What's the real truth?" "I'm a member of a cult and full membership in the cult requires that a member of the family or a loved one be offered up as a human sacrifice. Failure to meet this demand would be met with excruciating pain, torture and eventual death." Fr. Laport's heart almost leapt out of his mouth. His lips parted but not a word fell from his mouth. He was on the verge of shouting, "What!" but he stopped short, mindful of how fragile the situation was. The young man had just started to open himself up in a way that would eventually lead to his conversion and social rehabilitation.

Fr. Laport restrained his emotions and leaned forward toward Julian and lent him a much wider and more compassionate ear. By then, Fr. Laport had realised that Julian was in a very precarious situation. He was cornered on every side and he was well aware of the curses he'd called upon himself. He was now at the mercy of the cult, the law, society and even worst, his family. He wanted a way out. The asylum was for him a temporary reprieve, but for how long would that reprieve last? This troubling factor confronted him minute by minute. It was written all over his face; it was plainly evident. He was contemplating suicide.

A prolonged silence interrupted the flow of the conversation. The young man gazed at his stomach. He resumed the conversation and said, "I wonder what's going on with my uncle's eyes in there, Father. You think he can see what's going on in my heart now?" It was the last statement and question Fr. Laport expected. A shrug of his shoulders was the most appropriate response Father could think of. When Julian was asked why he'd eaten his uncle's eyes, he responded, "For more vision. That's what the cult told me but now I know I've been tricked, I've been fooled. I've been taken for a ride by the cult." Julian had been a vulnerable person all his life and in his search for guidance, had fallen into the wrong hands, where part of the cultic ritual entailed enduring the very form of physical abuse that had brought him over the edge.

"To whom shall I go?" he asked Father Laport. It was only then that Fr. Laport realised that Julian was a lone ranger who needed more help than appeared on the surface.

Sadly, he was a lone searcher. He had got lost along the way. Apart from being exploited by those who were meant to be his mentors, his own peers directed him onto the wrong path. He had read the wrong literature which had exposed him to the world of demons; his occult studies took possession of his faculties and transformed him from a person to a wild beast. He was obviously under a spell and the spell had to be broken. Besides this spell, he needed a great deal of counselling to help him overcome the problem of physical abuse which was responsible for his gradual demise.

With this experience and the experiences of Cane City behind him, Fr. Laport wondered what his ministry would be like in Boloville and Rest Town. He recognized now that the sequence and order of change depended not on fate but sometimes on the geographic location and the environmental conditions. Fr. Laport, at his point of departure for Boloville and Rest Town, left himself open to the will of God. Sadly though, Julian's opportunity was never extended to the accused in Bay-of-Ray. The young man from Bay-of-Ray was simply left to languish at the hands of the State. The State interprets such cases within the narrow context of Law or Psychiatry. Both Law and Psychiatry are devoid of a spiritual content and can be inadequate for a holistic diagnosis and prognosis for victims of such a nature. Julian, however, made a full recovery and re-entered society as a fully integrated person.

Chapter Eight

Boloville

Fr. Laport believed that Mother Nature's life cycle has been mind-boggling so far. She is the only woman to be born, to die and to come to life in the span of twenty-four hours. Her life, her death and her resurrection measure the brevity or longevity of man. It is believed that her re-enactment of birth, life, death and resurrection are lessons in wisdom for humankind. The lessons encourage all to cease the pursuit of the trivialities and tangibles of this life at the cost of their salvation. Mammon has made fools of many in past generations. It has deprived its victims of the wonderful opportunities to learn from the cycle of Mother Nature's journey.

Proverbially speaking, every man, woman and child have their moments of birth and rebirth. They have seasons of agony and death. The agony of some people is more prolonged than others. For some, there may never be a resurrection but only eternal death. The greed of humans can eclipse their chances of daylight and put them into a perpetual darkness. The sun will not shine for everyone at the same time, nor will darkness come upon all at once; yet there are many who are more fortunate than others. They will have the dawn to greet them at birth and the sun to guide them always. They, in turn, can be the sunshine in life for others; they can be the candle in darkness; they can be the angel of hope in the hour of death and the way to resurrection. Such bright spirits must be selfless.

Boloville needed a Good Samaritan who was willing to be that dawn, that sunshine, that candle and that angel. St. Maria and St. Pompinus Street may just have been the address where deaf men and women lived. Its dwellers never heard the cries of their neighbours' distress. They never heard the language of the oppressed or perhaps they were unable to interpret it. Their suffering neighbours were people who found it difficult to utter God's name but found it convenient to express themselves using expletives, while those in agony died without the joys of palliative care.

There, on the corner of St. Maria and St. Pompinus Streets, Antonius died heaped up in a corner drained of every drop of blood from his body. At the home of Antonius and his two sisters, Julienne and Carla howled, shrieked and mourned. The good people on St. Maria and St. Pompinus Streets never paid them any mind. They were written off as mental cases but rumour had it that their father was an incestuous pedophile. He had also gained himself a reputation as a soul trader. He bought and sold souls. His name was Jagkarib. His children were all zombies, soulless beings.

One day, Father Laport went to administer the last rites to a sick and dying individual who, in his feeble voice, said to him, *'Fadda, mwen ni an kwèsyon pou mandé'w.' Es an moun sa bay ében van lam'y bay an lot moun?* (Father, I have a question for you. Is it possible for a person to give or to sell his soul to another person?). Fr. Laport was stunned by the gentleman's question. "Why did you ask that?" "No, Fadda, is not me. It's Mr. Jagkarib who came to see me and he asked me to give him my soul. And if I don't want to give it to him for nothing, he is prepared to buy it from me for money." "What?" asked Fr. Laport, "Did Mr. Jagkarib really come to your home, at your sick bed and put this request before you?" "Yes, Fadda, that is what I'm telling you." "What did you say to Jagkarib?" Father asked. "I told him to go to hell. He's a damn fool." "You are perfectly correct my dear brother. God will bless you a hundredfold." Then Fr. Laport proceeded in the administration of the last rites. The man died at peace with God that same night.

As for Jagkarib, there was no end to his lunacy. It is believed Jagkarib sold the souls of all his children as well as his wife to the devil. There was never a silent night on St. Maria and St. Pompinus Street. Some ears were immune to the noise and slept through the horrors of the persistent pleas: "Leave me alone! Behave please, I'm begging you! Behave!" the girls cried all night. Like sheep, one by one, they were led to the burial ground under the cover of dark and laid prostrate on tombs where they were violated and various rituals were performed over them. Sadly, they feared death so they jealously guarded the secrets of their torture. The girls were quickly written off as demented freaks, but truth be told, they had begun life as lucid beings.

When Fr. Laport first came to Boloville, he peeped out of his window several times in the night to try and locate what seemed like a torture chamber hidden in a little backyard in what appeared to be a hovel. From that hovel, the voices of Julienne and Carla were heard howling, shrieking and moaning. All was pitched dark out there. Only the street lights glittered. Not a soul was seen on the streets. In the background, the waves were heard bashing against the canoes, beached on shore, while the rest of Boloville slept.

As the sun rose, Julienne and Carla emerged from their torture chamber, their faces bloated and their eyes were bloodshot from their sleepless night. As Fr. Laport made his way to church that morning for Mass, his eyes fell into Julienne's eyes. "Good morning. How are you?" he asked. Julienne gave a whimpering smile, "I fineeeee." A sympathetic look came over Fr. Laport's face. He wondered how a person in so much pain could claim to be fine. He hurried to the church with the deliberate intention that, on his return to the presbytery, he would stop and have a chat with Julienne and her sister.

As he was approaching the entrance of the Presbytery, Carla shouted, "Good morning!" Father Laport answered, "Good morning and I hope you are doing fine." Sheepishly, she bowed her head and with her hand over her eyes and mouth said nothing. At that point, Fr. Laport saw an opening to initiate some form of dialogue. Julienne immediately joined in. Both Julienne and Carla were extremely guarded over what they answered. Judging by the questions they asked, they were craving for redemption out of this situation; but before they could give utterance to their pain, Jagkarib appeared almost as if from under the ground. His head was bowed and his eyes were fixed on the pavement. A felt hat reaching as far as his ears and right over his eyebrows cast a shadow over his entire face. He shouted at the girls: "Get inside now." As if he were deaf, he paid no attention to Father's greeting.

Fr. Laport was unruffled. He was not deceived by Jagkarib's intimidating, deliberate, deceptive, slothful presence; all of which Fr. Laport knew was well orchestrated to gain the sympathy of the village folk. People had always been suspicious of his fugitive behaviour and in order to avert suspicion, he clad himself in a costume of false humility.

Fr. Laport had every intention of getting to the bottom of the problem of the house of torture. Night after night the howling, shrieking and mournful cries for help continued unabated. For days on end, Fr. Laport thought long and hard and wondered what Mrs. Jagkarib's role was in all of this. Rhetorically he asked, "Is Mrs. Jagkarib deaf? Is she just dumb or indifferent? Or is she just downright callous? Is she an accomplice in all of this drama? If she is not one or the other, why has she remained silent to the atrocities committed against Julienne and Carla?" After all, they are the fruits of her womb. She suffered to birth them. Had she surrendered to Jagkarib's lunacy and idiosyncrasies?

Any attempt to speak with Mrs. Jagkarib initially proved futile. Fr. Laport never gave up hope. He knew that the chips had to fall in place one day. He only had to intensify his prayer and fasting and be patient. The rest was squarely in God's playing field. While navigating these turbulent waters, past experiences had taught Fr. Laport that the worst things had sometimes happened for a good reason. Jagkarib was impervious to change and Fr. Laport knew he was walking towards the goal of self-destruction. Like Pharaoh, he was marching towards his final defeat at the Red Sea yet he would not listen. Not even persuasion on the part of God would stimulate his interest. History has taught that God has, in the past, kicked up storms and aroused oceans to redirect the idiosyncrasies of men like Jagkarib who would not accept his gentle mastery. Israel had to know the exile of Babylon before they could appreciate freedom and long for it through God's assistance. The drama of Jonah and Balaam's jackass bears eloquent testimony to this truth as well. Therefore, Fr. Laport hoped that one day, before his death, Jagkarib's heart would bend to God's will and that he would see his children as gifts instead of victims.

It was mid-morning. The sun was weighing down on Boloville. The pavements were sizzling. The asphalt was melting like wax. A meal could have been cooked off the pavement. Every blade of grass in Boloville was scorched. The bare hills and surrounding mountains were glossy with what seemed like raw sulfur.

From the corner of his eyes, Fr. Laport caught sight of two girls fast asleep on the hot pavement. As he approached them, he realized they were Julienne and Carla. Sweat was oozing out of their pores like an open shower. Their dresses were stuck to their bodies like stamps to letters. Their faces were drawn with exhaustion and dehydration. The whole night long almost until dawn, Fr. Laport remembered hearing Julienne and Carla howling and moaning and lamenting, calling for help. Regrettably, no one, not even Fr. Laport, had reached out to them. He watched them and saw how wasted they were by sleeplessness and nights of struggle. With the help of neighbours and passers-by, he arranged for them to be lifted off the sizzling pavement and carried into their home. Fr. Laport followed into the home. What greeted him was 'out of this world.' In a minute's walk he found himself in a different, primitive world. It was not a home; it was a sty. Sadly, he thought, it was humans that inhabited it, not pigs. Even pigs would have preferred lolling in a muddy swamp rather than spending time within the confines of these walls.

The walls were blackened by smoke that over the years had turned into a wax-like substance. The lone bit of furniture was a narrow bed. Every bit of fabric too had been stained by exposure to grease. The curtains were mere threads, too frail to be blown by the wind. The windows had all lost their panes. The floor never had the pleasure of seeing a broom.

Fr. Laport stood aghast. Silence had him under siege. The scene looked as if time had stopped since the Stone Age. The air inside was heavy and breathing was laborious. Fr. Laport felt his lungs were under attack. For a brief moment, he was forced to walk away from the house. By then he was visibly gasping for breath. He was asthmatic and he feared an attack under such circumstances.

On his return to the house, he said to Jagkarib, "These girls are going to the hospital today." Jagkarib's upper body undulated like waves. So violent was his protest that he shouted at the top of his voice "No, my daughters are not going to the hospital!"

Fr. Laport offered him no resistance. He calmly returned to the presbytery, got into his car and headed to the police station a few miles away. When he returned, he was accompanied by two officers. Father directed the officers into the house and they too were taken aback by the condition of Julienne and Carla, and the house as well. Fr. Laport requested their assistance to take the girls to the hospital for medical care and attention. They agreed.

Jagkarib again registered his disapproval and made a dash to get between the officers and the girls. Fr. Laport then raised his index finger, pointed it in the direction of Jagkarib and said, "You make just one more move and my fist will come down on your head like a sledge hammer. Then you will wonder what on earth fell on you. I will do everything I possibly can to "rearrange your ignorance" as

Paul Keens-Douglas says. Hearing this, he stepped back three paces. During all of this, Jagkarib never lifted his head. He never removed his hat and never looked anyone in the eye. All things about him were evasive.

The girls arrived at the hospital and careful examination revealed that there was evidence of molestation. All over their bodies were demonic inscriptions and marks of dedications to demons. It was Christmas-time and Jagkarib was desperate to have the girls back in the house. Fr. Laport would not allow this until someone investigated the matter properly but the police officers were reluctant. The mere mention of demonic activity was enough to intimidate them.

As for Mrs. Jagkarib, Fr. Laport had suspicions that she was, directly or indirectly, an accomplice in the drama. She'd been tight-lipped all along but, in every dilemma, there is always a last straw which breaks the camel's back.

While Mr. Jagkarib was always evasive, his wife was practical; she was profoundly secretive, to her own detriment. A battle over Julienne and Carla's admittance at hospital was being waged between Mr. Jagkarib and Fr. Laport. Much as Mrs. Jagkarib tried to distance herself from it, her husband would not permit her to. She was under extreme pressure to make a deal with Fr. Laport for the girls' discharge from hospital. She was now standing between the devil and the deep blue sea. There were visible signs that she was cracking up under pressure from both sides. Her husband realized that Fr. Laport was not an easy nut to crack. It was obvious to Jagkarib by then that they had reached a stalemate and Fr. Laport would not concede to their demands to bring Julienne and Carla back home unless the proper conditions were met. Besides, Father had promised him to bring down the full force of his fist on his head. Jagkarib was not willing to push his luck any further. He turned his attention to his wife and applied pressure on her to negotiate the girls' return. It was visibly evident that she was distracted.

Necessity brought her to Fr. Laport one day. By then Mrs. Jagkarib had grown weary. Her endearing heart could no longer endure more pain. The signs were there; she was under severe pressure from Jagkarib who demanded that she get Julienne and Carla back home by a specified day and time or else she and/or Fr. Laport would both die. Fr. Laport was not about to let that happen but her will was breaking under this pressure. Drenched in tears, she told the whole story: Jagkarib wanted the two girls back home in time for a blood sacrifice, a *black mass* on Christmas night.

"Oh! No!" Fr. Laport erupted. "That can't and will not happen. Julienne and Carla are already victims of nocturnal sexual molestation and God alone knows what else. Will you sacrifice them again?" "They are soulless beings," she confessed. "He's sold their souls to the devil," she admitted. It turned out that Jagkarib also was an avid reader of demonic books and that every night without fail, séances were conducted with the devil, both in the house and at the burial ground. The children, she admitted, had been held down by their own father to allow the devil genital privileges and she had often assisted him in the process. Even when it was he, Jagkarib, who was molesting the girls, she assisted by pleading with them to submit humbly and quietly to their father's demands. She admitted, Julienne and Carla were impregnated several times but the babies had never been carried to full term. By the time they were three months into the pregnancy, they were beaten mercilessly on their bellies until they were forced into a miscarriage. These aborted fetuses were used as communion sacrifices at *black masses.* Fr. Laport, by then, was getting sick to the stomach. He wanted to puke but he would not trust leaving Mrs. Jagkarib alone in his office. The conversation, though nauseating, was becoming unreal. Was it a cover up to justify her dysfunctional conscience when she said, "There are a lot more people involved in the cult, Fadda. There are persons in positions of authority who are in it. People as far south as La Trinité Island and as far north as Crab Island are part of the cult." Fr. Laport interjected, "Cult, did you say?" Her eyes widened as if it was only a slip of the tongue but she finally acknowledged, "Yes Fadda, it's a cult." "Of what use is this to you?" Fr. Laport asked. "You are living in dirt poverty!" She sheepishly admitted, "The devil promised us we will get rich, but first sacrifice all the children." Fr. Laport erupted. He slammed his right fist on his desk. He shouted, "You and your husband are perfect candidates for the grave. Age and evil have wasted your lives. When again do you expect to get rich? And if you do, who will inherit it when all your children are sacrificed? Can't you see both of you are fools?" Mrs. Jagkarib was dazed, as if she was just wakened from a very deep sleep. She searched desperately for words to defend her position but nothing was forthcoming. At that point, she realised she was losing the battle against Fr. Laport. She knew too, she was dead meat. By then, Fr. Laport had well understood that mammon was at the root of it all. Julienne and Carla were just mere tokens in the chess game of the cult. Hold on to your seats.

During this time, Julienne and Carla were making tremendous strides. The doctors and nurses, like Fr. Laport, were very anxious about their future. While they were old enough to make decisions of their own, the truth was that they were penniless and powerless. Dependence was the likely culprit to consign them once again to an insalubrious climate. They were already victims of that environment over which they had no control because extended family members and the wider community had, over the years, distanced themselves from the situation. Both extended family members and the wider community had considered them untouchables. Like the lepers of the Old Testament, what would be their lot? Would they have to be driven out of the community? Would they have to reside in the hills or in the forest or die a miserable death in isolation? They were vulnerable and needed as much help as possible.

There came a time when the hospital could not continue to keep them as patients. Jagkarib, unilaterally in the interim, had made plans to move Julienne and Carla to another house away from the eyes and ears of the public. He intended to continue unabated with his nocturnal rituals. The girls were discharged. Jagkarib, under the cover of darkness, sneaked them into the new house. The night had hardly run its course when the cycle of abuse had started all over again. The police, unfamiliar with the world of spirits and necromancy, were too afraid to cross into that territory. It was taboo country for them. Julienne and Carla, like fugitives, took refuge into the hills. They opted to live with the wild animals which showed them more sympathy than the man and woman from whose loins they were birthed.

Time and time again Julienne and Carla emerged from hiding. They came into the village to search for food. They walked side by side uttering not a word to anyone. Someone remarked *en passant*: "These two girls are the only visible ghosts I have seen with my own eyes. The only ones dressed in actual flesh and bone." Indeed they were walking zombies. By all accounts they had turned their backs on Boloville, and if at all they were disenchanted with the people of Boloville, they never bothered to utter it. If and when they glanced in the direction of anyone, their eyes were like glass marbles. They were transfixed and rigid, dazed and distant. They wore the eyes of the dead. It felt like their eyes were arrows looking with deadly intent. There was little anyone could do to help them. Not even Fr. Laport could reach them at that point. Their trust was dying with them.

As time went by, they became more and more elusive. Like rats on the run, they were desperate to save their lives from an unexpected intruder. Jagkarib eventually died. Mrs. Jagkarib lived on to tell the tale of an obnoxious legacy and to experience her hell on earth. Jagkarib's name lived on with the invocation of his name in the blasphemous *black masses* offered by the occult fraternity he left to mourn. Nevertheless, their story was not the only one. No! Gina's horror story was on its way.

Chapter Nine

Rosa Town to Helen Island

Having survived the turbulent waters of Boloville, Fr. Laport was under the distinct impression that he had triumphed over the iceberg. He looked forward to calmer seas and smooth sailing. That was before gale force winds blew in from the south, stirred up the waters again and caused another swirl around him. A huge battered ship was thrown off course into his path. Instantly, Fr. Laport realized that there was still a long and perilous journey ahead of him. The ship swayed from side to side in search of a safe haven. Every port of call ignored its SOS until Fr. Laport, in Félicitéville, responded to its cry of distress.

On board that proverbial ship were three visible passengers: Gina, Harria and Evita and as many as six legions of demonic powers, occult powers, principalities, astral assignments and backup spirits, sent against Gina to possess her, to torment her, to restrain her efforts, to break her alliance with the cult. Harria was Gina's spokeswoman. Every time the spirits took control of her faculties and locked her mouth and deprived her of divulging any information, it was Harria who spoke on her behalf. Evita was there as the bystander. Fr. Laport was their only audience but it was not a pleasurable position he wanted to occupy.

By then, the experiences of Solfatara Town, Bay-of-Ray, Potsville, Cain City and Boloville had taught Fr. Laport many valuable lessons on how to navigate the turbulent waters. However, he never dreamt that his journey would be intercepted by one like Gina's ship. As urgent as their SOS was, Fr. Laport had made up his mind that he would not adopt a reckless approach in such turbulent waters so as to arrive at a quick solution. He was adamantly determined to get to the genesis of the problem before he attempted any exorcism on Gina. Fr. Laport had met his first tsunami in the person of Gina.

Gina

Very early in the process, Fr. Laport had learned that Gina was only eight years old when talk of marriage loomed over her head. Her mother, Elfita wanted a suitable suitor for her. Gina knew absolutely nothing about marriage, yet her little heart recoiled in shame and fear whenever the topic of marriage was raised. The only thing her mother told her was, "Once you are married, you must leave the safety of your parents' home." For an eight year old child, this meant spending the rest of her life with a total stranger. The mere thought of this thing called "marriage" riveted her mind, heart and soul in fear.

Fearing the worst, Gina thought it best to run away from home in search of a more child-friendly environment. There, she would be able to grow up in peace, reach maturity and carve out a future for herself and her mother. Her father, she was told, had died before her birth. It was a wasted thought. She was just too young to run. Rosa Town was a tight-knit community, surrounded by miles and miles of forest. It was a hunting community and the inhabitants knew the forest like the backs of their hands. There was nowhere in Rose Town for poor Gina to hide.

Many of her attempts to flee were foiled. Either a bus driver, a pedestrian along the way, a hunter, or the police would physically take her back home. Eventually, she successfully made her way out of Rosa Town undetected. Gina soon arrived in Karol Town, on the East Coast of Guyabera. It was a rude awakening for her. It was first and foremost, a transition from a natural jungle to a concrete jungle. At least Gina knew her way when she was in the woods of Rosa Town. In the concrete jungle, Gina's nightmare had just started to unravel. Because the law was looking for her, posters of her face, with strange inscriptions below it, were plastered everywhere on the city walls. She had never seen such large photographs before. For a while, she wondered if the walls were mirrors. Wherever she went, her face appeared in the press and media. Repeatedly, she heard her name called over the radio described as a missing child and asking anyone seeing her to report it to the nearest police station.

Gina was found and given up to the law. Eventually, a woman named Gobolda, who claimed to be her father's biological sister, came forward. Gina was released into her care. Whether Gobolda was really Gina's biological aunt is still debatable. For it would be difficult to imagine that an aunt could be so ruthless and heartless. Poor Gina! The darkness she dreaded had only just begun.

Gina was hardly nine years old when she was forced into an early child-marriage to Ziptapis, a man much older than she. Gobolda and her household assisted in constraining Gina on the wedding night to be deflowered. Gobolda and Ziptapis feasted on the blood that flowed from Gina's loins. They were like hungry vampires. It was the first emotional blow in a long sequence of blows that Gina would later be subjected too. The poor child claimed she saw heaven, earth and hell that night. The next day she made a bid for a daring escape but the attempt was anticipated by her alleged aunt and her adult husband. She was intercepted and the attempt was foiled. Subsequent to her attempted escape, Gina woke up the next day to find herself in the company of Gobolda and Ziptapis, boarding a flight to Helen Island. The flight was airborne. Gina's mind was paralyzed. Fear of what was to come crippled her. Unlike other children, excited to visit a new country, Gina was instead cloaked in fear. At the back of her mind, she was convinced that she was marked for slaughter. Her vocabulary was too limited for her to think of it in terms of prolonged and routine victimhood but in fact that is where it was heading.

In Helen Island, Gina would soon face a series of brutal rapes under the guise of marital duties and obligation. Gina was also raped by women. Sexual experience was etched into her mind. As a stranger in a foreign land, and a child, she was in a terrible predicament. She thought, "How can this possibly be marriage?" There was no answer forthcoming.

Within weeks of her arrival in Helen Island, news arrived that Elfita, her biological mother, had passed away and that her father, Elford, whom she had earlier been told was dead, was alive and living in the United States of America as a successful businessman, although he had suffered a severe heart disorder. She tried to make sense of the news but her mind became more and more confused in the process. She made no sense of the *mêlée mélange*.

By then Gina was asking herself whether she was cursed on earth. Without warning, a voice from within said to Gina: "You were never born to be cursed." What was her purpose on earth? Was she born to be a sufferer? Certainly, life thus far had never been generous or gracious to Gina. All she had ever known was abuse, fear, pain and misery.

As for Elford, her father, whether he was really dead or alive, he was only a phantom to her. However, as Gina grew older thoughts of this bizarre story about her biological father and mother's demise haunted her. Somewhere at the back of her mind she did not believe a word of it. By then, she had started questioning the veracity and identity of Gobolda, but there was no way of finding out.

Elford periodically visited Helen Island from the United States. Whenever he visited, according to Gobolda, his daughter Gina was always conveniently out of state visiting her deceased mother in Guyabera. Gina and Elford's paths never crossed. During his last visit to Helen Island, Elford disclosed his plans to Gobolda. He intended to will his entire estate in the United States to Gina upon his death. The word had hardly dropped from his lips when Gobolda arranged a visit for both herself and Elford to see a young lawyer in Félicitéville. The conniving Gobolda had by then conspired with Ziptapis to make her biological daughter, Mariam, the heir of Elford's estate instead of Gina. Elford was duped. He was given documents as proof that Gina's legal name was Mariam. The will was drawn up in Mariam's name and that same night Elford died a very mysterious death.

By then, Fr. Laport had deduced that perhaps Gina never knew and may never know it was the love of mammon, the deception of Gobolda and the connivance of Ziptapis that was the foundation on which her gibbet stood. Gina was much too young to understand the language of victimhood and sacrifice. It never crossed her mind that she was a victim and a sacrifice to satisfy the greed of someone else. She was too young to recognize such manipulative actions to bring about her demise for the rise of another. Gina was only a means to an end. Gobolda had intentionally and Ziptapis had willfully conspired to claim Gina as Gobolda's niece so that they could make her their victim and sacrificial lamb. In the first instance, it was their intention to have their hands on the Elford's estate and in the second instance, for the benefit of a cult that was under the leadership of the same people. For Fr. Laport, all of this was horrible but for Gina it was just the tip of her iceberg and she wanted Fr. Laport to help her dissolve the monstrous iceberg with her. Her friends, Harria and Evita were determined to assist the best they could but they had not yet understood the entangled mess that Gina's life was in. Therefore, they believed that their meeting with Fr. Laport would be a simple abracadabra and Gina would be delivered from her legions of spirits. No! This was indeed far removed from the reality which confronted them and which Fr. Laport had to deal with.

Black Mass

Fr. Laport had gathered that when little Gina had escaped from her traditional Rosa Town; she was on the run from child abuse. Unfortunately, she fell into the wrong hands. Although Gobolda and

Ziptapis had promised the South American authorities they would protect Gina that was far from the truth. It was a gross oversight too on the part of the authorities. Instead, Gina was placed into the hands of a high priest and a high priestess who were farmers of human vineyards. The wombs of unsuspecting little girls and young women of child-bearing age like Gina were their treasure troves. As he listened to Gina's story, Fr. Laport coined the word "Grapevine" to define the notion of grapes, winepress and Eucharistic species. The wombs of young women were used by Gobolda and Ziptapis as vineyards to grow and to harvest the Eucharistic species needed for their *black masses*. At the tender age of nine, while still a sapling, Gina was forced to produce her first fruit for sacrifice.

Yet at that stage, Gina was unaware she was a grapevine and her womb was a vineyard. Religiously, she was raped and impregnated. Each time, about three months into the pregnancy she was brutally beaten over her stomach and forcibly made to abort the fetus. The fetus was collected into a basin. The blood was extracted and stored and the body of the unborn child was wrung until every drop of blood was extracted. The little limbs were sliced or diced into tidbits as gift offerings and communion sacrifice during some ritual which Gina was forced to attend. The participants drank the blood and ate the flesh. Gina's mind could not fathom what was going on. The whole thing, she thought, was repulsive and obnoxious.

That was the first time Fr. Laport had heard such gruesome details of the *black mass*. Mrs. Jagkarib had raised the subject *en passant* with Fr. Laport when she negotiated the return of Julienne and Carla to Boloville but it was just glossed over. It was then that Fr. Laport understood the gravity of the agony of Julienne's and Carla's souls.

Gina considered Gobolda and her devotees as devil's incarnate. They were wicked, malicious and gross. In short, they were cannibals and blood suckers. To put it more succinctly, "They were vampires," said Gina. Gina had no idea what a cult was at the time. All she knew was she never wanted to be part of this thing where people ate the flesh and drank the blood of humans and witnessed unusual demonic and spirit manifestations before her eyes. The impact of such drama was much beyond the capacity of her mind and the tolerance of her stomach which made her puke again and again without compromising her repugnance towards such rituals.

The older Gina got, the more her life descended into chaos. Her mind felt as if it had been pinned to a rack; it was a mass of confusion. Her soul was in utter torment; her world was hell; her body felt like a bloody abattoir. Her womb was like a necropolis without headstones. Her integrity, her self-esteem were no more. Her mere appearance was itself a contradiction unable to be penned in words or utterances. If indeed the eyes are the mirror of the soul, then a peek into her eyes would tell it all. Her soul was languishing within.

There was a cry for help, a cry for vengeance, a cry for redemption and deliverance. Though alive, yet her soul screamed much louder than the blood of Abel. From within her conscience, the unborn spoke with abundant clarity. They too wanted redemption. Gina, while still alive, was their only hope of redemption. Night and day, the cries of those restless souls, her unborn children, tormented her. She longed for death but the voiceless screamed within her souls, "Hold on until we have been redeemed." Meanwhile, with flattering tongues, Gobolda and Ziptapis did all within their power to convince Gina to dismiss her conscience and concentrate on the value and dignity of being a chosen one.

By the time Gina had reached her sixteenth birthday she had endured many rapes and at least thirty-five abortions. Gina birthed three children, only because during these three pregnancies, she went into hiding. However, their lifespan was brief. The cult's demand for new born flesh and blood did not give them a chance to live. Their lifespan was shorter than that of ferrets and far less than their appearance on a stage. These lifespans were like floating debris swept away in turbulent waters. Her children were her phantoms. Was it all visions she'd been having? No one could tell. Her dreams and visions were not pleasantries but rather her experience of hell on earth.

Fr. Laport listened attentively to the horrors of Gina's dark night of the soul and wondered how in Jesus' name an individual could endure such horror for so long. Neither her soul nor her conscience ever rested. Her mind was a perpetual caldron of unquenchable fire. Her mind was in a permanent state of vacillation between the devil and the deep blue sea. The restless souls of her dead and aborted children spoke to her. It was they who told her that she would forcibly be inducted into the cult.

Shortly thereafter, Gobolda gave Gina an ultimatum, "Become a member of the cult or you'll face the consequence of death." By then Gina was old enough to make her own decisions. At least, that was what Gina thought; but with her mind vacillating between the devil and the deep blue sea, freedom was not hers to take. The world's largest boulder stood before Gina and she was challenged to break it with the smallest hammer – her body. Her body and her will were not her own. Gobolda possessed it all. Gina's chances of escape from the cult without outside intervention were limited. The possibility of her mind being distorted by friends was also thwarted by Gobolda who was like a sentry on duty twenty-four-seven and she would never have permitted it.

To be sure that there would be no outside intervention to aid and abet Gina's defection, Gina's education was put on hold; and she was never permitted to venture too far from home or the yard where they lived. In spite of all the safety measures Gobolda put in place to draft Gina into the cult, Gina, of her own volition, never consciously surrendered to Gobolda's demands. She never consented to the cult's initiation rites. She never wanted to be part of this blood-drinking and flesh-eating thing. It was too gross. Nonetheless, she awoke from sleep one night to find herself restrained by four hefty men: her body lay flat on the floor in the posture of a cross; her wrists slit and her blood oozing from her veins into a basin placed in a well-carved hole in the floor. One by one, each individual in the circle had their wrists slit.

All the others in attendance voluntarily shed their blood. All the blood was later mingled one with the other, then poured into what looked like a chalice. In turn, each member took a sip from it and ate a portion of the aborted fetuses harvested from other young women like Gina. While they chanted their mantras and followed instructions from a big black book, then from the Secrets of the Psalms, they followed instructions for the lighting of various coloured candles as they heaped maledictions on their enemies. Gina nervously stated that her most frightening experience at these rituals was the arrival of Gobolda's husband, Satan. Fr. Laport by then was praying under his breath. He was praying for Gina and for his own safety. In his flesh, he felt like Peter walking on the turbulent waters. From time to time, he shifted his focus from the Lord to himself and, at such times felt as if he were sinking; but in his spirit, Fr. Laport felt the tenderness of the Lord say to him, "Courage my son! It is I! Do not be afraid! I am with you! Pay attention to Gina's plight just for my sake and I will redeem her in my appointed time."

Fr. Laport returned his full attention to Gina's story. "Satan," she said, "comes amid smoke and burning flames and his demands are always met. Once Satan comes, the devotees evoke all the wicked spirits and the spirits of the dead, and they command these spirits to take possession of their bodies to torment the lives of their enemies and to bring ruin and disaster into the lives of their unsuspecting victims." The veracity of such atrocities was already much beyond Gina's comprehension.

During the course of the conversation, Fr. Laport discovered that Gina had never been baptized. She had never been instructed in any Christian tradition or faith but Gina's conscience was very much intact. She still had some notion of right and wrong, good and evil. In her own unique way, she was not prepared to succumb to evil. Her undeveloped conscience did not permit it either but it was no easy task or struggle on her part. It was an eleven year war waged with Gobolda and the cult. Gina was determined that Gobolda and the entire cult would fall at the end of the war but not herself. She, Gina, was determined to be the victor in all of this.

Fr. Laport reckoned it was eleven years and counting and Gina was ineffectual in her efforts to break the bond Gobolda had created between them. The harder she fought, the deeper she found herself falling at Gobolda's feet. 'A worrisome thing,' she thought. Gina was convinced she was under a spell but spell or no spell, hex or whatever compulsion she was under, Gina knew within her the time had come when all things had to be broken. Within her soul, she denounced the rites of initiation performed over her against her will. Her firm conviction was that the initiation held no sway over her. Gina was determined to free herself from the grip of the cult. According to the teaching of the cult: "Unless a person of his or her own volition eats the flesh and drinks the blood of the newborn and unless the initiates of their own volition swear against the name of God and Jesus and partake of the sexual orgies with all members of the cults (both male and female), they cannot become full fledge members of the cult." Gina assured Fr. Laport that up until the time she had spoken with him, she, of her own volition, had never consented to the rites that had been imposed upon her. Gina knew that once she had accepted initiation into the cult, she would be killed as a human sacrifice when she was no longer needed as a grapevine. It was for no other reason that Gobolda impressed on Gina's mind she was the "Chosen One". In plain and simple language, Gina was chosen to be a human sacrifice from the day of her birth. Fr. Laport's mind by then was overwhelmed, but Gina's heart was like a buoy in turbulent waters. It was the marker to guide Fr. Laport in the direction Gina's exorcism would go and so he had to let her heart be open to tell her story.

Realizing what was on Gobolda's mind, Gina did all humanly possible to deflect Gobolda's powers. The harder Gina tried, the harder Gobolda and other cult members stepped up their efforts to maintain and tighten their grip on Gina. In their last ditch efforts, when Gobolda and other cult members realised that she was being helped by Fr. Laport, Gina was placed under the direct power of some more deceptive spirits, other than the legions which were already assigned to her. Those wicked spirits spoke and thought on her behalf and often sealed her mouth whenever she was questioned on any subject concerning the cult and their trafficking people.

By then, the war had moved past the battle of mind and body. It was a war against spirits originating from the kingdom of darkness; those who could not be fought against with mere flesh and blood. The talk by then was spiritual warfare. This war had to be fought with truth, integrity, the spirit of the Gospel, the shield of faith and salvation and the word of God from the Spirit, to use as a sword (Eph.6:14-17).

Having listened to Gina's dilemma, Fr. Laport realised that for a long time Gina had been a one-soldier army. From Fr. Laport's perspective, Gina had all along been a pretty strong one-soldier army for a long time. In other words she was a Samson in a needle. Weakened, yes! Blinded for a while, yes! Surrounded by enemies, yes! Despite all else, Gina was a firm believer in divine justice and that Gobolda's coliseum would one day fall upon her and her cohort.

Among the spirits who controlled Gina's life was the spirit of her late mother, Elfita. Initially, Gina claimed there were as many as thirty-five spirits who from time to time took possession of her body and faculties. Elfita and her cohort of thirty-four spirits pretended they were good spirits and had taken possession of her to guide her away from the cult. However, those who knew Gina knew it was indeed the contrary. Every time Gina obeyed those spirits, the water round her grew more turbulent. Harria and Evita were misled into believing that Elfita and her cohort were good spirits up until the time when they were led to the brink of depravity.

Elfita was evidently the master mind of the lot. Deceptive as she must have been in life, she was in death. Elfita misled one of Gina's friends and confidant, Harria, into believing that Gina's problem stemmed from the fact that she had never been baptized. It was not the baptism which mattered at all to Elfita. In fact, the baptism was intended only as an act of mockery for anything sacred. From sacrament to sacramentals, anything that's blessed or consecrated must be desecrated. God, Jesus, the Holy Spirit, the Church or his anointed ones must be demeaned by Satan, his angels and devotees. And his devotees too were ruthless in their blind submission to the devil's will. Their hearts were bent towards the largesse promised them without a thought of its consequences.

With Elfita's plans detailed to the tee, Harria arranged for an appointment to visit the parish priest of Stone Town, Fr. Alfred Paul, to make the necessary arrangement for Gina's baptism. By this time, Elfita had possessed Gina's body and had weakened her to a near death condition: a condition which appeared as if Gina was more in need of the final rites instead of baptism.

However, there were preconditions laid down by Elfita to be followed before an appointment with Fr. Paul was made. Harria and Evita were required to accompany Gina to the point where the river met the sea. At that location, the three were told they must first engage in all forms of sexual acts possible both on land and in the sea and under the water with Gina to create a bond between them to make the sacrament of baptism more efficacious in Gina's life.

Undoubtedly, Evita was taken aback by such a ludicrous request. At first, her head shook nervously at the sound of the request. Then she asked Elfita to explain to her the connection between the efficaciousness of the sacrament and the sexual orgy. Elfita quickly responded through Gina, "The transmission of bodily fluids during the acts would help establish a Christian connection between Harria, Evita and Gina and in so doing, prepare Gina to receive the sacrament worthily." Sadly though, in their ignorance and desperation to help Gina out of her predicament, the two girls became victims of Elfita's wickedness.

Elfita's deception did not stop there. She went further to ensure that Harria and Evita would be well grafted into her snare. She encouraged them to sleep with Gina and to share more body fluids for a period of one week before the day when Gina would be baptized. In the interim, Gina had apparently taken a turn for the worse. This time, Harria was forced not only to advance her appointment with Fr. Paul but to invite him to Gina's home to administer the Sacrament of the Sick. That was not to be. Fr. Paul visited Gina on her sick bed. When Fr. Paul arrived, Harria proffered the opportunity to speak with him separately, away from the hearing of Gina. She explained Gina's predicament to him and the many struggles she had been through over the years and that it was her desire to break away from the cult. In the process, Harria used the opportunity to put her cards straight. She divulged to Fr. Paul the preconditions Elfita had placed upon her and Evita as a pre-requisite for the efficaciousness of the sacrament for someone who wants to be set free from the claws of the cult. Fr. Paul just couldn't believe the simplicity of Harria and Evita. On hearing this, Fr. Paul fell backwards against the wall. "What!" He shouted. "That's bull's crap!"

Fr. Paul immediately demanded that they denounce such idiosyncrasies. He pleaded with Harria and Evita to denounce and renounce such demonic beliefs and such depraved actions. He further impressed upon Harria and Evita, as well as Gina, that if such instructions were ever followed again, Gina would be denied the Sacrament of Baptism. By this time, Elfita had placed Gina on the brink of the grave in an effort to solicit the generosity of Fr. Paul, as it were, to baptize Gina.

His mind and heart initially were not given to what appeared more of a ploy rather than a genuine need for Gina to be baptized. But Harria and Evita's incessant plea bent his heart and Gina was baptized *in extremis* on the premise that if she recovered, she would receive the full baptismal rites of the Church. Gina subsequently regained her bodily strength and followed a Pre-Jordan course in anticipation of the full initiation rites one Holy Saturday night during the Easter Vigil.

Elfita wanted Gina's baptism for her own ends. Despite all their efforts and sacrifices towards the efficaciousness of Gina's baptism, Elfita also intended it to create doubt in the minds of Gina, Harria and Evita. In other words, she intended the baptism to disprove the power of God. She wanted to create doubt in their minds as well as to weaken their faith. It was then that all hell broke loose and the demons launched a swift and persistent attack on Gina. They made her life a living hell. A zombie is too mild a description to define her state. The spirits who once claimed they were "good spirits" showed their true colours. From within and without Gina was mentally, physically and spiritually tortured morning, noon and night. The spirits had not anticipated that Gina's baptism would have precipitated the beginning of their destruction. They had it all wrong. All along, they believed they would have used Gina's baptism for their own ends. Instead, it turned out to be the contrary.

The spirits claimed Gina was a deceiver. She had rejected them by not following their dictates leading up to the baptism. In other words, what was communicated to Gina secretly and what was conveyed to Harria and Evita were at variance with the spirits' expectations. Elfita was a chip off Satan's block, a deceiver to the core. However, Gina was prepared to get Elfita and her entire cohort of spirits out of her life once and for all. Regardless of the cost, Gina wanted to break bonds with them.

Elfita refused to depart. Instead she fortified her forces, took up residence in Gina's body and claimed it as her own. She persistently tortured Gina and weakened her but Gina's desire to see Elfita go did not wane. Weakness or sickness did not deter Gina in her efforts to expel Elfita out of her life once and for all. Gina continued her fight but Elfita lingered on. She punched deeper wounds into whatever was left of Gina's vulnerable conscience demanding answers for following the directives of Fr. Paul which had affected the counsel of her legion.

Gina was determined to swim against Gobolda's tsunami. She was just as determined to renounce the cult and to free herself from the grip of the spirits. Gina was not prepared to be a grapevine any longer. She was determined to put a stop to her womb being the tomb of her unborn children. Gina's resistance put Elfita's efforts at the crossroads both with Gobolda and Satan himself who had long-term plans to make Gina his personal bride as promised him by Gobolda, in Gina's presence. Elfita turned up the heat on Harria. She and her legion initiated and waged a silent war with Harria, leaving Evita as a spectator, only to torment her, and break her will so that she would later encourage Harria to submit to the demands of the spirits. But what Elfita and her cohort did not know was that Evita was made of a different fabric that was not easily torn.

Harria herself was a product of steel of a different kind. She was deceived once by Elfita's deception. Harria was not prepared to be a victim a second time. No! Not Harria. She was prepared to take the fight a notch higher each time the situation demanded it. Harria, of her own volition, assumed the responsibilities and duties of a foot soldier to fight side by side with and for Gina. Evita stood shoulder to shoulder with Harria at all times. They took the battle head on;

they stood ready to confront things both visible and invisible and to ride every wave with Gina together.

Harria knocked at every door where she thought help may have resided. Many doors opened and closed in her face but that did not deter her efforts. Harria was restless. She had spent her very last penny. She was bankrupt, but bankruptcy did not deflect her efforts or flag her zeal; it did not change her mind. Day by day the tsunami intensified. Elfita and her legion of spirits took it one notch higher each day. Emotionally, spiritually, physically, occupation wise and even on an economic level, Harria was weather-beaten. Evita was not too far behind in this regard. Their lives were restless to the point of exhaustion but they never conceded defeat. No! Not them. They were like Roman fortifications within themselves. Their faith took them where the flesh was most reluctant to follow and in slow measure they were weathering the tides.

In reality, Elfita recognised that the cult's grip on Gina had weakened with time. Elfita and the members of the cult had miscalculated the impact of the Sacrament of Baptism on their presence in Gina's body and on the cult itself. It dealt them a severe blow that was not readily visible to the naked eye. Thus, even Harria and Evita were unable to discern the Baptism's positive effect in this regard. At that instance, Elfita, Gobolda and the cult members had felt its adverse effects for the cult. By then, Elfita turned to Gobolda and the other cult members for assistance. Together, they geared themselves for further open warfare on Harria and Evita, using Gina as their open target.

They had recognised too that Harria and Evita were Gina's strength and their move was to weaken them or even eliminate them regardless of the financial cost to the cult. Gobolda made no bones about it. She wanted Harria and Evita dead. Gobolda went so far as to arm Gina with the smallest, yet most lethal dart, a poisoned thorn blown through a bamboo stem to kill Harria. Gina knew the effectiveness of that weapon well. She knew too that if she had used it on Harria, no doctor would have been able to diagnose her cause of death. It was the cult's secret weapon. Gina's conscience did not permit her to use it on Harria because she had recognised that Harria was indeed a loyal and true friend, one who really wanted to see her deliverance from the cult and who worked towards that end with great zeal. Gina was therefore not prepared to put her only soldier and general down. Instead Gina dug a hole, buried her secret weapon, placed a twenty-five cent piece over it and buried it too. That was the price she was paid to eliminate Harria.

Spirits, it has been said, know the actions of men but cannot read the minds of the living. When the spirits and members of the cult understood that Gina had deceived them in this regard, the cult members posted foot soldiers at every angle, hoping to trap Harria and Evita. Instead, the Lord was working on Harria and Evita's side. Many times they were victims to the deceptive spirits' *bull*, but they were never conquered. As the battle intensified and Harria's resources, energy and human resource levels fell lower and desperation set in, temptations came in torrents. All Harria and Evita wanted was Gina's deliverance. They were prepared to do whatever it took in faith, to see the end of Gina's malaise but Harria's determination had taken a toll on her and so her discernment was left limping in her exhausted footsteps. Evita's faith was still flagging but her weakened frame told it all. That was the loophole Elfita and her cohort longed for. They wasted no time in capitalizing on this lapse. Unknown to Harria and Evita, Elfita pulled new tricks out of her old bag and made the same offers clothed in different garments. It was a situation which Fr. Laport had predicted all along but at this point, Harria thought she was invincible. That was a very serious *faux pas* on her part.

Now sufficiently weakened, frustrated and worn out, Elfita and her legion were out for a field day with Harria and Evita. Gratification and depravity were only a stone's throw away. Harria and Evita were both thrown into an entangled mess of concupiscence and massive disenchantment with themselves when they discovered that their suitors were members of the same cult, who were working in collaboration with the same doctors who performed their abortions.

The doctors themselves were also members of the cult but in their desperation to assist Gina, Harria and Evita were made to realize that they had been grapevines for a while. They felt defeated and betrayed. Guilt overpowered them for a while. Without a second thought, they repented with a firm purpose of amendment. With the assistance of Fr. Laport, they opened themselves to the Sacrament of Reconciliation and did the same for deliverance from the cult to deflect any relationship established in them but unknown to them. Side by side with Gina, they submitted themselves to the rite of deliverance and saw themselves through.

The Lord speedily came to their rescue and saved them from the hands of the enemy but not without serious repercussions from the cult. The Lord did not allow then to stoop a third time to the same depth of promiscuity and depravity which, according to Gina, were acts leading to initiation into the cult membership.

The spiritual warfare for the deliverance of Gina inflicted an indelible wound in the flesh of the cult. They were not prepared to concede, nor were they prepared to allow any further infiltration into the cult. Gina's defection meant the divulgence of pertinent information and secrets. Too many of the so-called bourgeoisie in every social stratum in Helen Island would be brought into ill-repute. Their duplicity would be real dirty laundry. The social structures would themselves crumble in want of total cleansing. In other words, the very structures of evil would be compromised. No! Certainly, that was a serious indictment Gobolda and Satan himself were not prepared to deal with.

A dictum was issued: "No member of the cult, under any condition, pain of torture or a slow death, is allowed to divulge secrets pertinent to the cult or attempt defection at any given time. Membership is a lifelong commitment." While the dictum was directed mainly at Gina, it was aimed implicitly at Harria, Evita and all those who assisted in Gina's defection. Gobolda, faithful bride of Satan, reminded all present: "The same applies to all members." Following Gobolda's dictum, a moratorium was placed on Gina's activities. All interactions with non-cult members were frozen. Members of the cult were willing to pay anyone a hefty sum to eliminate any non-members who kept company with Gina or who tried to guide her along the path to full deliverance. Even Fr. Laport and Fr. Paul were considered villains in this respect. They too had death sentences hovering over their heads.

The warfare persisted. Gina repeatedly went in and out of trances. Was it a defense mechanism on her part? Perhaps no one would ever know, but Gina, in the interim, did assume a multitude of personas and spoke in various voices challenging and intimidating everyone who dared to lure her away from the cult under such circumstances. The intimidation took on several forms: revealing personal and hidden secrets, personal issues pertinent to the life of spouses, job related issues and personal problems of the past. Whatever it took to intimidate and keep others away from Gina, the cult put it into full effect.

Harria and Evita received repeated death threats but Harria, the more persistent of the two, just would not surrender although she had been on the verge of victimhood on numerous occasions. As hard as Harria tried, Gina's victimhood persisted unabated. Gina's rape and impregnations were like recurring decimals. Her body had become a rag for the cult members. Her beatings and abuses were merciless.

It was mid-morning when Elfita took control of Gina and revealed to her that she was pregnant. That same night, an initiation rite was scheduled. Elfita warned Gina, "Brace yourself for a brutal beating. Your baby will be the sacrifice tonight." The vision, the dream or the possession had hardly ended when some members of the cult walked in on Gina. She was lying in her bed. The room was in utter darkness. The party, who walked in on her without warning, verbally abused her. Then they turned on her and physically beat her almost to near death for untold reasons. They then all walked away, locked the door behind them and left her helplessly in bed with no food for the rest of the day.

Despite all the physical abuse, there was never a mark, not a single thread of evidence left on her body to confirm the veracity of Gina's claim. Yet Gina was, in fact, physically abused and her pains were, in fact, real. It was Elfita who, on several occasions, told Harria it was useless taking Gina to doctors as they could never diagnose her pain and besides – they too, the cult had its agents planted in the health system in the persons of some doctors and nurses. On that note, Elfita was correct. Gina was generally weakened by the beatings, but there was never a trace of it on her body. Yet her body reeked with pain. The slightest touch had Gina recoiling into her body. She screeched like a wounded elephant at every touch of the part of the body where she was beaten.

Emotionally wounded, Gina retired into bed. The one thought which rummaged through her mind was, *"The death of another child and the blood sacrifice which is pending this night."* She knew too of Gobolda's apostles' arrival in Helen Island from South America, Crab Island, Warlock Island, La Trinité and Montgomery Island, south of Helen Island to be part of the initiation rite. Their high priests and priestesses were expected as well from South America and Crab Island. The local fraternity of priests in the cult would concelebrate with their visiting counterparts. Gina held on tenaciously to her last thread of hope: that her baby would not be aborted and that she would be exempted from the said ceremony.

Just at that time, Harria telephoned Gina to enquire about her. Gina emptied her cup of sorrows on Harria's already overburdened shoulders. God bless Harria! She drank it sip by sip until Gina's cup was emptied. When the cup of sorrows was emptied, a brief silence followed. Then Harria invited Gina to pray with her over the telephone. They prayed the Holy Rosary together. In the process, Gina was hit with a bout of excruciating stomach pain – a pain which mimicked birth pangs, something that she had been so familiar with even before she knew what puberty meant. She tossed and turned hoping for the pain to go away. Then suddenly, she went into labour. It was another miscarriage. Another bunch of grapes was ready for vintage and sacrifice. Elfita reminded Gina, "Your womb is our vineyard, bitch."

Elfita was right. Gina's womb was the cult's vineyard. Each pregnancy produced a cluster of grapes to be harvested in time for producing the wine for the sacrifice. Shortly after the fetus was birthed, someone walked into the room and collected the basin. Its contents were taken away and prepared. It was the newborn blood and flesh the cult needed for their sacrifice. Sad but true, Gina was not exempted from the rite; she too had to eat and drink of her own flesh and blood. Gina saw herself as a tomb within a tomb. To put it more succinctly, her frail body, worn out by misery, was a limbo for unredeemed souls, fruits of her own womb. Talk about a walking garrison, it was Gina's body. In conversation with Fr. Laport, she described herself as an abattoir. The butchers were the cult members. Chief among them was Gobolda whose marching orders no member in the cult would dare disobey. Everyone in the cult knew she was Satan's personal bride of choice. They all trembled at the sound of her voice which had a thunderous ring to it.

Gina had come to realize that her body was a sanctuary of unredeemed souls and spirits. Her body was a shrine where those who had not yet gained access to the world of the redeemed would cluster within her, hoping to find redemption by way of her defection from the cult. Eight years of enslavement seemed like an eternity in hell for both Gina and the deceased children. Her soul had become their tabernacle. There, in her soul, the unredeemed took refuge all at the expense of Gina's peace and well-being. She was a prisoner within her own body. Yet the unredeemed showed by their actions that their preference was Gina's imprisonment, her bondage; never their own redemption. They possessed her will. They were determined that her destiny was the dream of their unfulfilled destiny. Gina was no longer her own person. Even though she may have lived in her own flesh, worn her own features, her soul, her spirit and her will were not her own. Those spirits controlled and dictated her every course of action. Even her relationships too were under their control.

The Silly Season

By then Ziptapis had eluded Gina and returned to South America to keep the momentum of the cult on a high note there. Fr. Laport learned that Gobolda had commissioned him to go back to South America to recruit other vulnerable girls like Gina as possible clients for the cult as vineyards. The demand for *black masses* was high and so too was the demand for newborn blood and flesh. However Ziptapis' absence did not put a halt to Gina's rapes and battery. They continued unabated. Gina had to be one of the cult's grapevines and they were not prepared to let her off the estate. The cult needed a constant supply of newborn blood and flesh. Besides, the silly season was approaching and *black masses* were in high demand. Gobolda would not let any vine on that estate wither, die or be uprooted; that would put a serious dimple in her stipends. Gobolda would never go down a broke woman or priestess. Of course, Gobolda's clients were more ruthless than Gobolda herself. They were a desperate lot. The reins of power were the only thing on their minds. They were Christians by day but conscienceless creatures by night. Under the cover of dark, their souls were compromised in preference to their transient goals.

Influenced by the alleged spirits, Gina started losing control of her faculties. The few people from outside of the cultic circle who dared to befriend her were alarmingly confused by her continuous spells, trances and the messages she claimed she was receiving form her deceased mother and her hosts of spirit friends speaking through her. They wondered if at all she was a medium of some sort. Soon their lives were an entangled mess and the hubbub which invaded Gina's life by the quick succession of events had infiltrated their respective lives as well. Desperation and panic were like clarion calls echoed in their voices. That was what motivated and spurred them into every direction in search of help for Gina. Even that too was a form of deception. They were themselves falling apart at the seams and were clueless as to how far they had fallen. By then, they were virtual victims of her dreams and visions. They too were becoming servants of the so-called good spirits, almost their devotees and servants without knowing that they were almost in the doldrums.

The veracity of her revelations and predictions all seemed like comedy and tragedy in a single act: a drama with a unique character and with so many actors, visible and invisible that it seemed almost impossible for its audience to know precisely what to expect in any of the acts or scenes. The drama of it all reached its climax without the last curtain drawn.

The Human Sacrifice

The night was dark. The dogs from every quarter howled like wolves. Some whimpered like mournful babies in bitter agony. The atmosphere was frozen with tension. Something seemed amiss. What was it? Out of the blue, Gina broke into a sweat: her voice changed; her eyes transfixed; her body quivered under the weight and impact of a column of smoke which walked its way into her body right in the presence of Harria, Evita and Fr. Laport. Their blood ran cold. Fear crawled over them like a hurricane. They were almost brought to their knees. Immediately they invoked the name of Jesus and mustered some strength and courage to regain their balance. Just then Gina shouted, "O Mount Koko, altar of human sacrifice. Their fate is sealed with thy greed, O great Gobolda. Your spouse, Satan, has granted thee thy wish. Two innocent souls shall be the grapes for thy wine and for thy sacrifice this night."

Initially, Harria, Evita and Fr. Laport thought it was all gibberish. 'Perhaps another of Gina's delirious episodes,' they thought to themselves. But no! It was not. It was instead another pure astral projection – an out-of-body experience. In the body, Gina was present to Harria, Evita and Fr. Laport but her spirit, her soul was there at Mount Koko. In her out-of-body experience, the spirits had revealed to Gina: a night had been set aside for a special blood sacrifice. The hour was approaching: there was a shortage of newborn blood and flesh. The promise of mammon was in the air. Gobolda was determined; she was not prepared to let that bundle pass her by. She must fulfill her promises. Her *black mass* had to go on. Nothing would stop her and her cohort. Greed was in total control of her wish list. Therefore, anyone was her likely victim and sacrifice. Gobolda summoned Satan himself and offered him as many souls as possible on the premise that her demands were met. Of course, Gobolda's demands were Satan's delight and pleasure. After all, she was his favourite bride in this part of the globe. At a glance, Satan spotted a bus of mourners *en route* to Félicitéville. He roared with laughter and shouted, "It's yours for the taking."

Within seconds, the stench of sulfur weighed heavily over Morn Koko. The residents of Morn Koko held no responsibility for the diffusion of this sulfuric gas. In fact, it was a puzzle for all of them. No one in the community had farted. It was not a volcanic eruption either. What was it? It was the legion of Gobolda's wicked spirits poised like hornets ready to launch their assault on their unsuspecting victims and carry them over the altar of sacrifice in anticipation of the scheduled *black mass*.

Without warning, the legion of wicked spirits slammed into a bus driver. They immediately took full control of his body, his soul and consciousness, and led everyone on board to their unprovided death. The heart-wrenching cries of those onboard did nothing to break the will of this legion. The babies on board disappeared from the scene in a flash without a trace. They later arrived at Gobolda's temple in Solfatara Town under the cover of dark in time for the blood sacrifice. Gobolda roared with laughter. Contentment was her joy. Her plan was executed to its finest detail. Helen Island was plunged into a state of panic. The nation was gripped in mourning. All minds were engrossed in speculation. The bodies were still warm and it seemed as if they had passed seconds before arrival at the temple. The attendants wasted no time. Within minutes, they were busy wringing out blood from bodies, dismembering and dicing them, preparing them for the sacrifice.

When all was ready, Gobolda and her cult summoned her new initiates. The initiates themselves were a desperate lot. They were prepared to descend to any depth to achieve their ends. For this sorry lot, depravity spelt success; grace and truth were unnecessary encumbrances. Nothing was going to prevent them from sacrificing their own souls. They arrived one by one under the cover of dark. Each one was extra cautious to protect his or her identity. They were purposeful in trying to escape public attention and to avoid any consequent backlash that would surely rob them of their intended goal just days away.

Their punctuality for the midnight blood sacrifice could never match their regularity at the altar of the Lord, if it were not expedient to their cause and personal selfish ambitions. Of course, some of them were already friends of Satan and were quite familiar with the procedures of the ritual. Some of them had already sacrificed the fruits of their wombs for favours on previous occasions. For the neophytes, the ripping off of a human heart while still alive was a real revulsion of the stomach and they were not able to keep human flesh and blood down their throats and so were forced to drink a second or third time. Otherwise, they would not be in total communion with Satan and the spirit world, and would, in turn, be victims of their shattered dreams. By then, they had withdrawn their baptismal promises. They similarly renounced the use of conscience to become mere tentacles of Satan and of the cult in high places.

Oh! dishonorable men and women, a sorry lot indeed they were. Unconscionable charlatans living comfortably, simultaneously on two sides of the fray without remorse, believing that once their hands bore no stains, they could not be held accountable for the demise of others. Of course, they had already lost their sense of the omnipotence and the omniscience of God and were totally oblivious of the words of the Psalmist, David, who assured Israel, that neither night nor darkness, depth nor altitude could conceal humankind's activities from God. Not even the unspoken word can escape the knowledge of God (Ps.139). Yet *ad lib* they dance with the dancers, sing dirges alongside the family and friends of their victims, then weep with mourners, without a hitch. The dancers and mourners are victims of deception disguised as truth and empathy.

Up until that point, Gina's mind was still in a quandary. Her underdeveloped conscience had difficulties processing the ambivalence and the deception of the devotees of Satanism. The same persons she saw worshipping Satan, communing on the flesh and blood of humans, partaking of the sexual orgies, desecrating sacramentals and engaged in abominations in the sanctuary of Satan were the very ones who were recognized by different names in various capacities in the churches, even men of the cloth and those who trample the halls of power with immunity from travesties of all sorts.

Revelations

Gina veritably admitted to Fr. Laport, "I'm unable to discern between the deception and power of the spirits and veracity and the power of God. Really, it is another troubling twist to an already perplexing drama with far too many scenes. I want to get out of this. My cup of sorrow is filled to the brim." With these words, Gina's eyes sunk deep into their sockets and her tongue grew heavier by the minute until she went into a deep sleep. Meanwhile, her throat contracted and expanded like the muscles of a weightlifter posing before an audience begging for more and more drama. Without hesitation, Fr. Laport bound the spirits and ordered them to depart from Gina and cede their place to Jesus. A long fifteen minutes elapsed before she could emerge from her sleep as Fr. Laport repeatedly sprinkled her with holy water. Then without restraint, and as if in a trance, Gina broke into a monologue with the spirit of Elfita. Her voice was audible as she spoke the following:

You came to my house twenty-five times
You took me to your *black mass* fifteen times
You beat me all my life
You took me and had me to strip in clubs eleven times
You cut my hair eleven times
You took my children away all the time
You've killed all of them
You prevented me from praying
You always confused my memory
You made me forget everything
You made my tongue heavy when I wanted to talk

You inflicted pain on me every day
You have held me down for as long as I have known myself, to be
    raped both at home and during your *black masses*
You took my money away all the time
Everything I own you took away all the time
You've used me to seduce my ex-boyfriends to join your cult
You used me to get people's information
You used your evil powers to take over people's souls
You repeatedly took over my body. I want my freedom
You took my mother away from me and you killed her
You killed my father
You took all my children
You beat my children out of me and caused miscarriages to get
    blood and flesh for your sacrifice.
And you, Gobolda and Satan, have destroyed so many innocent
    lives just for power and fame.
Satan is a deceiver.
God is at my side.
God is at my side.
Jesus will save me.

Then a struggle ensued and Gina came out of her trance. She fixed her eyes into Fr. Laport's and he asked, "Who were you talking to?" "Elfita," she replied.

"Wow! What a confession!" Fr. Laport thought to himself. Other than the spirit of Elfita and her cohort, the spirits of Gina's deceased children were her constant harassment. Their cries echoed in her ears night and day. Like Abel, their blood cried minute by minute for vengeance. The torments were hers to bear. They had become her cross. She was on a personal never ending journey to Calvary. She felt their souls within hers. They were like prisoners crying for release. Even if they were put on parole, they would have preferred that instead of languishing in torment for the sins they had never committed. They longed for their redemption. Their plea, every cry for help, was of itself another nail for Gina's crucifixion. Gina's anguish was beyond her point of endurance. Her back was against the wall. Gobolda had pushed her against the wall and the souls of her unborn children as well as those who were killed, were anchoring her into the wall. They demanded her to do what she was unable to do of her own accord without the help of faith.

Gina at one point opted for death, but her eldest daughter who was birthed told her that the Lord was not ready for her as yet. If she, Gina, should die in her present state, she would be in more torment than she was already. She claimed that the daughter had pleaded with her to seek her own redemption first. It was at this point that Elfita requested Gina to ask her friend Harria to assist her in receiving baptism in the Catholic Church and she, Gina would find redemption. Did that trick, pulled by Elfita work? No. It did not. If at all, it may have just precipitated a barrage of attacks on Gina's life and turned up the heat of Harria's confusion and demise.

A Soldier's Dilemma

At this point of her journey with Gina, Harria felt as if all avenues had shut down on her and she had slammed her face against a stone wall. There was just nowhere to turn. "Desperation," she said, "is too mild a word to describe my fright mode." Her fright could not be expressed in words. Of course there were visible signs of this written all over her body. Her eyes were on the verge of popping out of their sockets. Ruts were dug deep into her forehead, her face drawn with exhaustion and her lips wrinkled with the constant toss and bites of stress. Her speech was heavy with despondency. Her shoulders were languid and her arms were lazy, not with intent, but worn out by fatigue in her wish to articulate Gina's story, and her needs in her predicament and that of Gina. Her heels were raised as if she were in a constant galloping mode. Her sweat glands seemed like reservoirs. Sweat streamed from the scalp of her head to her feet. Harria's body had grown somnolent by then and help seemed to have distanced itself way beyond the horizon.

Yet, despite her state of despair, Harria's resilience would not let her body be gratified by sleep while the enemies, the spirits gained ground and further devastated Gina's life. From all indications, Harria was determined to storm heaven and bring God down to earth by any means possible. "St. Michael, I think," she said, "must be either on vacation or he must have had his fill or he has been fired by God. He's not listening anymore." Every priest she had consulted to seek assistance from, took her round and round the mulberry bush and finally pretended they had no recollection of who she was or of the case. It was by then a case of resistance versus resilience. Which of the two would be victorious?

Gina's Quandary

Gina's quandary was mind-boggling. On several occasions while in her sleep, Gina was transported to unknown destinations. On numerous occasions, she woke up in various parts of Helen Island miles away from her home: sometimes stark naked and penniless; other times she woke up in the bed of total strangers. The latter had placed Harria beyond her limits. As for Gina, her dilemma had placed her at a precarious mountain surrounded on every side by gullies with their throats as deep and wide as the valleys of death. Gina's only way out of there was to be either airlifted or, willing of her own accord, to journey with someone who was willing to guide her to the best valley where she would be safe. She had to be prepared to undertake yet another painful journey on foot back to the valley. Harria was prepared to take the journey with her.

Gina's most daring experience was one New Year's Day when she was cooking with Gobolda and she felt exhausted and went to take a rest. The next thing Gina found herself doing was travelling from Stone Town to Félicitéville with six hundred dollars in her pocket, a quantity of money she had never seen or ever held in her hand before. Consciously, she stopped the bus in Boloville and took another bus back to the Stone Town. The next thing she remembered, she was near Félicitéville. Later that same afternoon, she found herself as the lone occupant on a yacht in the middle of the Caribbean Sea. How did she get there? She was clueless. She swam across and made her way back on land. Harria by this time stumbled across the name of Fr. Laport.

Chapter Ten

A Cry for Help

Good health by then had not been very generous to Fr. Laport. He had had quite a battle with ill health himself over a few years. There were tons of speculations about his health condition for which Ma Pépé from Cane City was held solely responsible. Her threats against his life and, of course, her loud mouth made her fully culpable. The opposite was true. Fr. Laport may have just over extended himself and overspent his energy and, in so doing, contributed to his first heart attack at the age of thirty-eight. Fr. Laport may have been overly ambitious when he undertook a parish-wide crusade from January to April of that year on five consecutive evenings per week. By mid-April, while preaching a sermon, he was struck with a massive chest pain and a temporary blackout which had him leaning over a nearby table for a while as if in deep thought. No one suspected – at least that was what he thought. As soon as he regained his strength, Fr. Laport laboured along until the end of the session that night.

The next day a teacher confronted Fr. Laport and demanded that he visit the doctor. The diagnosis was not what he expected and early retirement was imminent after frequent bouts of the same. However, Ma Pépé imposed this on herself because she made no bones about it; she wanted Fr. Laport dead. Her daughter and son were partners in crime.

It was just seven o'clock in the morning. Fr. Laport was still doing his morning devotions when the telephone rang. "Hello, good morning," he answered, "Can I help you?" The person at the other end of the line introduced herself as Harria. She wanted to make an urgent appointment to see Fr. Laport. Not knowing the full details of her situation, he graciously extended an invitation to her to meet him two days later at nine-thirty in the morning. Whatever Harria and Fr. Laport had spoken of on the telephone and what they spoke of when they met in person sounded so distantly related that, by the end of their first meeting, he had second thoughts about a second meeting.

For all intents and purposes, his initial reaction was to say to Harria, "I'm afraid this is much beyond my scope and my health will not endure it." Compassion had him thinking otherwise. He extended an invitation to meet with Gina in person. By all accounts, Fr. Laport expected to meet a hag. On the contrary, an angel appeared before him. The only things which gave her away were her eyes and her looks. They were the epitome of gloom and doom; indeed an angel from hell itself. Her eyes were glazed; they were like over-pitched marbles. They were dull and sank deep into their sockets.

As soon as she was directed to take a seat, Gina, like a peeved child, sank as deep as the steel-seat chair permitted her to. The odds were against her. The chair was another measure of restraint. Gina fidgeted with the chair for a while and then voluntarily admitted there weren't any further adjustments to conceal her. Self-protection was the next item on Gina's agenda. Her vulnerability was evident; her mistrust too, was self-revealing; her bodily posture was a nonverbal yet explicit confession of a life riddled with ordeal after ordeal. Gina exhibited every sign of a prisoner within a prison yet not confined to a prison cell. Gina's fetal posture told her life's story. She was the bearer of a deep-seated wounded ego. Her body was a temple for asylum-seeking souls. Thus, it was quite obvious that she was unprepared to open herself for fear that she would reveal the identity of her asylum seekers who, over the years, had shown no mercy towards her but instead had only inflicted her with wound after wound.

Throughout the interview, Gina sat sideways. She maintained that fetal position to the end; that was her security blanket. To help further shield her wounded self, Gina clasped her hands against her chest. She pressed her index fingers hard against her lips. They were symbolic padlocks placed on her lips. She never uttered a word. Her eyes were fully dilated. Her irises looked like dry graphite, projectiles well poised to hurl across the room unannounced in her defense. Her eyes carried the most austere look that Fr. Laport had ever seen in his life.

From time to time, she glanced at Fr. Laport from the corner of her eyes. The poor priest, his butt riveted to his seat, had the strangest impression that Gina was determined to nail him to the wall with her eyes. He described them as: her hammer and her nail. The scary part of this encounter was her most befuddled look. Fr. Laport said Gina reminded him of a cornered rat - a rat with only two options: play dead and still be struck a fatal blow or scamper out of the room in search of safety only to be caught by a ruthless hawk. At all costs, Gina had one thing on her mind: protect her badly damaged ego and bedraggled look. In her best defense, she assumed the characteristics of a comatose tetanus patient; her lips were sealed; rigor mortis had set in. Harria was her voice; Evita was the lone spectator throughout the interview.

After the first interview with Fr. Laport, the tables had turned topsy-turvy on Gina, Harria and Evita. The gates of hell were torn down and there were seemingly two separate residences: one where Gina lived and the other where Satan had set up his throne. By then, Elfita had assumed a new persona. She was no longer Gina's mother nor was she Gina's guardian angel anymore. She then called herself Pyonica. The good spirits all seemed to have taken leave of absence when Fr. Laport had commanded all the souls by name to return to the Lord for their just judgement. In came Pyonica, the queen of terror. It was she who oversaw the rapes, impregnations, the battery and the miscarriages. It was Pyonica who tried to conceal Gina at *Fon Jan Lib* where she woke up on several mornings. Other times, Gina found herself stark naked sheltered by a colony of pigeons.

On one occasion, Harria and Evita spent almost an entire night in prayer with Gina. It was about eleven-thirty in the night, when they made their exit but not before they had bolted every door and window. Early next morning, just before dawn, Harria was awakened by the sound of the telephone. It was Gina. She was calling from Solfatara Town. She was sitting at the jaw of a caldera, stark naked with blood oozing from her loins. The last thing Gina remembered: she was in a trance; there were chants all around her. As she spoke, she remembered Pyonica, Gobolda and a number of bourgeois from Félicitéville as well as others from various parts of Helen Island who were there as participants. They were chanting, swearing in the name of Satan and saying, "This is my flesh! Eat it! You will have power! This is my blood! Drink it! You will have power." When she saw blood oozing from her loins, Gina broke down in tears as, by then, she'd realized her vine had been harvested. Another *black mass* had been celebrated and she was still a victim of this wretched cult.

Over the telephone she asked Harria, "When will it end?" Harria was lost for words. She begged Gina to be patient and promised her that she would call Fr. Laport to arrange another meeting. Gina's question made Harria feel totally inept and powerless. Poor thing, God knows she had tried for three years to find help for Gina but she was left to fend for herself like a jilted lover whose lover was too timid to journey with her because of his own inordinate fears. Harria mustered her strength, embarked on the journey to Solfatara Town and brought Gina back home to Stone Town.

Pyonica and Gobolda, threatened by Gina's precipitated move to break her alliance with the cult, grew relentless in their efforts to stall the process of deliverance. Their attacks were frequent and subtle. It was beyond the imagination of Harria and Evita to anticipate from which side they would suffer the next bout. As for Gina herself, her body had become a hornet's nest. Sleep evaded her. Her earnings disappeared without a trace. Her telephone was tapped and intimidating messages were transmitted over it to Harria's phone, Evita's and all customers with whom she conducted business; a business which was already on the brink of collapse. In the face of all these developments, Harria contacted Fr. Laport and told him, for a second time, desperation was too mild a word to describe her efforts to rescue Gina. When words are not minced in such troubled times, it means victims are cognizant of their predicament and may be worried about the turn of events.

Victims searching for a way out of their misery operate on the premise of expediency rather than of principle. An over-exuberant individual looking for recognition as an exorcist is an ideal prey for the devil's snare. He or she is the devil's entrée. It is better to err on the side of caution than be a victim of self-conceit. Urgencies are not always emergencies. Tangibles can be dealt with expeditiously. In the world of spirits, prudence and deep spiritual preparedness are assets. A profound spiritual preparation is the spine that will sustain one through the process of an exorcism. Be careful of the plea of the victim. It is the greatest of temptations to act with haste. Be on your guard against victim sympathizers. They too can tempt someone to act with pride to turn stones into bread at their demand. Wisdom has it: tread as gingerly as possible. Grace, Faith, Discernment and Wisdom are your best friends and weapons; rely on them. Haste is your worst enemy; avoid it but do not overlook it. Fr. Laport was determined not to overlook the principles of discernment and spiritual preparedness.

Fr. Laport never intended to ignore Harria's plea on Gina's behalf. However, in his discussions with Harria, he recognised that Pyonica and Gobolda had become more audacious and rampant in their attacks on Gina. In fact, their efforts and attacks had grown tentacles, to say the least. Fr. Laport was not at all surprised when Harria told him that she was beyond desperation. Her desperation had to be read in its proper context. Harria had been on the run for over three years.

She'd knocked on many doors. Some opened up halfway but many were closed to her face outright. Thus, when she caught hold of Fr. Laport who gave her an extended listening ear, Harria did all within her power to get that fish to swallow bait, hook, line and sinker until it was beached and finally landed on her dinner table. There was no way she would let that fish bite off the hook or line and swim its way back into the open ocean. Once that fish was landed, Harria wasted no time. She wanted immediate attention and action. Interviews and all else were just unnecessary paraphernalia. Harria wanted an immediate exorcism for Gina but Fr. Laport impressed it upon her that discernment is a key factor here. He himself needed to wait on God. Prayer, fasting, reconciliation, penance are also imperatives which must not be overlooked. Proper spiritual preparation is an absolute before any exorcism can be done. In times of crisis, the talk of preparation seems like a foreign language much beyond the comprehension of victims and sympathizers. Never- theless, in the interest of all participants in such drama, the longest way is the best way to take. There is an axiom in Helen Island which says: shortcuts, short lifespan; long road, long lifespan. That's the only thing in Fr. Laport's book that was and still is neither myth nor legend. Experience has taught him so.

Victims, their family, friends and sympathizers are part of this preparation too. The entire household must also be spiritually prepared. They must be prepared for any further eventualities during the preparations and during the exorcism itself.

Appropriate novenas, prayer, fasting and penance are mandatory especially for those who wish to be witnesses or participants during the rite of exorcism. No doubt, preparation time is usually the most difficult, especially for the victims. Gina was no exception to the rule. Following a visit with Fr. Laport, Gina, Harria and Evita were commissioned to pray a deliverance prayer nine times *per diem* covering themselves in the blood of Jesus and asking the spirits, by name, to depart from their lives. It was no surprise to Fr. Laport when Harria, during the course of that week, called and reported they were under attack. Gina, who was at the time pregnant, had once again lost another baby. She was beaten mercilessly and the fetus was forcefully ejected for the cult's ritual sacrifice. By this time, a new actor had emerged onto the stage. The drama enrolled new characters all the time. Or did some of the old actors assume new names and new personas?

Enter Manitus

Manitus, was a new adherent to the cult. He assumed the rights, duties and privileges Ziptapis once held over Gina but he was no parallel to Zitapis. Manitus was an incarnate feral beast fitted with feral instincts. In his hands, Gina was mere forage. He was indeed one of the finest architects chosen by the cult to accomplish her dehumanization, demoralization and impoverishment. On average Gina conceived four times per year. In between each pregnancy, she lived on a diet of physical and ritual abuse. He confiscated her last penny while she squirmed in misery at his feet. Mercy evaded her cry for help. The spirits who purportedly had come to her rescue, only made matters worse for Gina. They were wicked, evil spirits, supportive agents of Manitus who were sent by Gobolda to take control of Gina's faculties and subject her body and mind to more damming and despicable conditions. Under the influence of these damming spirits, lies, deception and abuses were all that emanated from Gina's mouth; enough to anger Manitus and to justify the cause for his brutality. Night and day Gina was tormented. Each day more and more soldiers joined the squadron of tormenting spirits.

In the latter part of this cycle of abuse and torments, Phillippa and Tyra, the two worst culprit spirits, took up residence in Gina's body. They confiscated her food, apparel and her money. They deprived her of sleep and led her into deep forests. They distorted every word uttered by Harria and Evita and blamed every misfortune and mishap on Harria and Evita, eventually achieving their goal: enmity, frustration and mistrust reigned between Gina and Harria and Evita.

It's believed that the spirits had become high tech savvy. Phillippa and Tyra were sending text messages via the cell to Gina. Such text messages resorted to name calling and character assassination. Gina and her deceased mother were classified as prostitutes. Gina was convinced Harria and Evita were the responsible sources of the abusive text messages and that further eroded her trust in both of them, thus forcing Gina, as it were, to find refuge in Manitus as a trust worthy confidant. Manitus too, guided by the counsel of tormenting spirits, was determined to see the end of the friendship between Gina, Harria and Evita. This trio was bad news for the survival of the cult. The friendship was seen by the cult as a definite link to sever Gina's affiliation with the cult. The cult lived to destroy the friendship at all cost. Therefore, whatever went wrong between Gina and Manitus, they blamed it on Harria and Evita.

Each time Manitus administered his ritual beating to Gina, he convinced her it was out of necessity that he did so. He was Gobolda's slave. He simply obeyed orders. He did whatever he was told and repeated whatever he was asked to say. Manitus did not know he had been robotized by the cult. Therefore, he *ad libbed* convince Gina that Harria and Evita commissioned him to physically abuse her for her lack of submission to the wishes and demands of the cult. However, the truth was that Manitus' administration of abuse on Gina was all at the behest of Gobolda. He was simply their agent and he did not know it. His conscience had died and he functioned on a make-believe emotional roller-coaster to convince the girls that he was more of a wimp than a brute. What he had refused to confess was that he was a whip in the hands of Gobolda, used for the humiliation and destruction of Gina to keep her loyal to the cult under all conditions.

By then the charade had ended for Gina. She wanted out of the cult and the constant abuse and battery had made it even more evident that she must leave; she must make her exit, alive or dead. The determination to make her exit was there but the way out was the most difficult thing to determine. That too was Harria and Evita's dilemma. Their lives had become more and more frantic in search of answers and a way forward. It was as if life had suddenly reached a cul-de-sac for Harria and Evita. It looked like even God himself had given up on them. Nevertheless, their faith was strong. There was no way for them to be contented to be in the cul-de-sac. They knew deep within them there had to be a better way out. Nothing would stop them from discerning that way, even if it meant taking their case before Archbishop Lawrence. All they needed was help from someone who was willing to journey with them.

It looked like frustration was the fuel which sustained Harria's energy. Certainly her heart was a heart of flesh. Only a woman with a heart of flesh understood the language of compassion as Harria did. Pyonica, for her part, knew Harria was made of steel, but her heart was flesh; so Pyonica was determined to transform Harria's heart into a heart of stone. But, Harria would not let her. She maintained her heart of flesh even when it was bruised at its worst. In one of her desperate efforts to bring Harria to her melting point, Pyonica led Gina to a strip club in Pretoria and had her to dance stark naked in full view of everyone present. For three whole days Gina was subjected to such debased actions at the behest of Pyonica. What made Harria even more empathetic towards Gina were Gina's multiple personalities. Harria was never sure when it was Gina or one of the many spirits who acted or spoke through her. It is said, "Necessity is the mother of invention." In this case, it was out of necessity that Harria and Evita had to invent a coping mechanism to help them deal with the whole charade. They learned to read Gina's eyes.

Foot soldiers are in no shortage in the service of the cult. Their resourcefulness in recruiting initiates surpasses the dynamism of best evangelists and sometimes enlists even some evangelists into their membership. The cult made no bones about it: they hated Harria and Evita as much as they despised their efforts to remove Gina from the grip of the cult; yet their hatred was in many ways a distraction to conceal their motive. As the saying goes, "If you can't beat them, join them." The contrary was true: "If we can't destroy them, recruit them."

From the very beginning, Gobolda had every intention of recruiting Harria and Evita as members of the cult by encouraging the two young ladies to engage in sexual relationships and sharing of bodily fluids as if to break the spell cast on Gina. That was a decoy. It was meant to strengthen the bond between them and Gina and gradually draw them into the circle of the cult. It was by sheer grace and faith on the part of Harria and Evita, who frequented the Sacrament of Reconciliation, but were counselled to do otherwise that they escaped the claws of Gobolda and membership into the cult. However, the devil was and will be forever relentless in his efforts to reach his targets. He will pursue them into the desert and make them the most lucrative offer just to mislead his victims into his sway.

When the efforts of Pyonica, Phillippa and Tyra failed to break the will of Harria and Evita, a new apostle by the name of Hilton, was recruited in another bid to solicit the good will of Harria and Evita. Hilton was a gigolo. It was not long before Harria understood he was a human sponge. Like a maggot, he fed off Gina's misery and the victims of the cult under the guise that he was a good-will ambassador, sympathetic to the victims of the cult. On the contrary, he was a bold-faced liar. He was *de facto* an agent of the cult.

From the beginning, Harria tried to arrange a face-to-face meeting with Hilton to discuss Gina's predicament but to no avail. Instead Hilton chose the easier way out: he spoke with Harria over

Gina's phone. Hilton did everything possible to convince Harria how much he loved Gina and was prepared to put his neck on the block to save her from the abuse she suffered at the hands of Manitus. Hilton repeatedly begged Harria to help him open a path to Gina's heart. No sooner had Harria facilitated his fancies than Gina was in his claws. Hilton turned from man to beast; his true colours unfolded. The gentle lamb had become a fierce lion. The moment Gina had stepped into his den; his claws pounced deep into her vulnerable flesh. The language of love and seduction had changed into the language of abuse and the dynamic of the cult's gambit was visible both in his utterances and actions.

Once again, Harria was daunted. She had failed Gina once more; yet she was still unsure that Hilton was a member of the cult. Her only concern was that Gobolda, with all her necromancy, or maybe the spirit of Elfita, or some other spirit might have been the cause of this sudden change of heart and behaviour on the part of Hilton. It was only by the slip of the tongue that Harria was rudely awakened to the reality that Hilton was indeed a professed member of the cult. He was indeed influenced and controlled by Phillippa and Tyra who insisted that he should never meet face to face with Harria and Evita. Otherwise, he would be considered an infidel by other members of the cult and thus, he would lose his potential status both within and without the cult. They convinced him that Harria, in particular, would ruin his future.

Was Hilton malicious or just naïve? Having said that much to Harria, Hilton further confessed that Phillippa and Tyra had asked him to marry Gina during a *black mass*, but first he was obligated to drink the blood and eat the flesh of Gina's recently harvested fetus. The cat was out of the bag; Harria was no longer in doubt. She knew for certain that she had been taken for a ride. Indeed, she had unknowingly betrayed the trust Gina had placed in her. At the thought of it all, Harria felt the full weight of her own anger and betrayal pin her to the wall. Her mind was wavering between anger and empathy towards Hilton. "Why empathy for Hilton?" she asked herself. After all, he too had betrayed her trust. He had seduced her into believing he was genuinely pursuing a relationship with Gina to help her out of her *malaise* but he was a liar to the core.

Harria just did not know what to think. She did not know what to believe. For a long time, Harria found comfort in her own philosophy: there is deception everywhere; but somewhere in the midst of all the chaos, there is an element of truth. Vulnerable as she was, Harria was left with little discernment on her own to discover where exactly that element of truth really was in the midst of the chaos. She had landed herself and Gina into deeper trouble while thinking help was on the way.

Her mind and heart were once again locked in a new dilemma: 'How would she ever rise from the consequence of her myopia, sequestered by her internal struggle to see the dawn of Gina's redemption?' Harria blamed herself. She just could not believe that she had allowed Hilton to seduce her into such a blatant betrayal like that. He'd undoubtedly played on her emotions all the way. Even if she saw him physically abuse her, his constant cry for help and his constant refrain was: 'He did not know why he abused Gina so much when he knew deep in his heart he truly loved her.' But such utterances were no less than blatant lies. They were simply decoys to conceal his true identity as a member of the cult and his definite aim was to delude Harria in order to place Gina firmly back into the hands of Gobolda and the cult, courtesy of Hilton. However, fate and deception are irreconcilable partners; deception's lifespan is limited by fate.

As hard as Hilton tried to stay clear of Harria, fate had it that they must meet. News circulated that there was a dynamic pastor by the name of Uzoboth in Félicitéville. He was blessed with the charism for casting out devils and evil spirits. Harria was advised by some sympathizers to Gina's plight to let Gina pay him a visit. Deep within her gut, Harria convinced Evita it was worth the while to take Gina to see the Pastor. When Gina entered the Pastor's office, she immediately recognized Hilton whose real name was Uzoboth. However, Pastor Uzoboth kept a very straight face hoping that neither Harria nor Evita would make the connection.

Gina went livid; she was hysterical. She put up a tantrum demanding that she be taken away immediately. Instantly, the spirits locked her mouth but her mind was as lucid as could be. Harria and Evita were quite perplexed. For a moment, they thought it was the spirits who were reacting to the presence of the Pastor. No! It was not. Gina had come to recognise it was Hilton; he was her abuser, her rapist, operating under the different name of Pastor Uzoboth. Hilton was indeed his cult name. 'By Jove, the man is a pastor' Gina told herself. Her mouth was sealed and unable to speak to reveal the deception and dilemma which stood before them. She knew her life was in imminent danger. How in Jesus' name was she going to get out of this trap? She was clueless.

'Gosh!' said Gina, "Hilton is a Pastor." Disbelief seized her for a long time thereafter. Still, her behaviour was incomprehensible to Harria and Evita. All they knew was that Pastor Uzoboth carried significant clout in Félicitéville and beyond. He was an acclaimed evangelist and exorcist. People believed in this man as a man of God. Many had skipped ship and had come over to his flock for the sake of his dynamism. "How can that be? No! It can't be," Gina thought. She recalled too, that she had seen him on numerous occasions in attendance at the *black masses.*

For a while, she doubted in her heart and mind that he was the same person until she recognized the *black mass* ritual sitting on his desk. No sooner had he opened the ritual than all the symbols used in the ceremonies of the cult popped right out of its pages. Gina froze; she kicked up a storm. Once again she recognised that her life was in profound danger. She demanded that Harria and Evita take her away, please. They however sided with Pastor Uzoboth. They were convinced that the devil and the spirits were resisting his presence and deliverance but Gina knew they were as wrong as wrong could be. Sensing something was amiss, Pastor Uzoboth immediately turned to Harria and Evita and chastised them for the crucifix they carried on their chains. He claimed it was a pagan symbol which impeded the process of deliverance and the same applied to any jewels they wore at the time. Immediately, he relieved them of their jewels on the premise that he would melt them and have them made over into something worthy of their Christian status. To this day, Pastor Uzoboth has no recollection of the gold chains, earrings, bangles and rings. In fact, he claimed that he has no recollection of the said event and if there was ever an occasion where he did meet with them, then Harria and Evita and the other young lady who remained nameless should come to see him privately in his office. Of course all three of them flatly refused by saying, "Oh no. Not over my dead body!"

It was at this point of blatant betrayal that Harria remembered the words of Fr. Laport: "This thing calls for prayer, fasting, penance, and a great deal of discernment. Failure to wait on the Lord to act in the interest of all in the battle of the world of spirits will lead to the path of self-destruction."

As Fr. Laport prayed over Gina, the spirits' stronghold was weakened more. Bold and disquieting revelations were made. It was more than just fetuses used in the rituals. Live babies too were sacrificed. Children, still alive, had their chests ripped open and their hearts ripped off their bodies. Devotees who conceived mainly for cultic purposes concealed their pregnancies to full term. They were aided and abetted by medical personnel who were themselves members of the cult. The babies were delivered on the altar and were sacrificed right on that same altar. Their throats were slashed as soon as they took their first breath. These harmless souls were hung by their tiny legs like dead chickens on a production line until the last drop of blood was drained from their lifeless limbs.

Gina was perpetually perturbed by such gruesomeness: the acts, the battery of young women, the orgies, and the barbarity with which the new born babies were slaughtered by so called people of honour and so-called Christians who held no qualms about their duplicity, believing that all who were in the circle were there voluntarily. "Pathetic, pathetic," poor Gina lamented. Tears drained down her cheeks. Mucous flowed down her nostrils like lumps of dough. Intermittently, she choked on her own words as if inhibited by the spirits. But no! It was not the interference of spirits this time. For as hard as the spirits tried, they were inhibited by the consistent prayers offered up by the prayer team and at one time pleaded with Fr. Laport, "Tell these idiots to stop praying."

No one paid them any mind other than to tell them, in the name of Jesus, to be quiet and to depart in trembling to the feet of Jesus. In the interim, more and more confessions were forthcoming. Gina's body started to sag. Fr. Laport was in deep empathy with her. He understood her pains and trials. Thus, he gave her a few minutes to rest and to catch her breath. When she emerged from her moment of rest and broke her silence, her weak voice uttered, "Look at my state; look at my condition; I am a victim. I was running from the pot and I landed in the heat of the fire. I have known hell all my life. Father, how far do I have to go again for me to meet Jesus?"

Finally, Gina had come to realize she was indeed a victim. Yet sadly though, she did not understand that she was not responsible for her victimhood. All she needed to know was that she'd been a victim of her ethnic traditions with which her soul was in conflict. She was ambitious for something greater than child marriage. She'd envisioned a greater and better future for herself and in turn, to help her mother find her way out of the poverty of the forest and jungle life imposed upon her and all her ancestors. That vision was definitely inhibited. It had been held back by Gobolda and Ziptapis who saw Gina as a grapevine for their cult but her spirit never surrendered. Her rebellion, though justified, was the cause of her misery. The cat was out of the bag and Fr. Laport felt it was time to initiate the rite of exorcism. This was no storm in a teacup. It was far worse than that!

It was a Thursday morning and Fr. Laport had a nine-thirty appointment with Gina, Harria and Evita. The time had come and gone and there was not a word of the whereabouts of this trio. At ten-thirty only Harria and Evita arrived. Gina had gone missing from the previous night. The two ladies looked haggard. Disappointment was written all over their faces. Somewhere in the back of Fr. Laport's mind, he expected something like that to happen. He knew it. He knew that if Gobolda and the other cult members had any wind of the exorcism, they would make it impossible to find Gina.

In fact, they knew and Gina confessed it. The members of the cult hid her deep in the woods and tortured her through the night. The following day, Friday, they showed up unannounced. Fr. Laport knew then he had no choice but to work with Gina when time permitted. His prayer team was summoned and, without hesitation, they responded positively and hastened to the place where the rite was to take place. Members were briefed of their duties and responsibilities and were left before the Blessed Sacrament. Fr. Laport, Harria and Evita accompanied Gina to a secluded room for the first stage of the rite of exorcism.

Chapter Eleven

The Rite of Exorcism

F
r. Laport was cognizant of Gina's dilemma: all her pregnancies were terminated against her will. The three children who were birthed were human sacrifices much against her will as well. In other words, they were never given a chance to experience the fullness of God's glory and redemption. Throughout the interviews, as Gina narrated her woes and encounters with her children's spirits, the response given by St. Paul to the Corinthians resonated in Fr. Laport's mind. When the Corinthians asked about the predicament of those who had died before receiving Baptism and the possibility of their hope for salvation, Paul responded by inviting the Corinthians to receive Baptism on behalf of their ancestors so that the ancestors might have a share in the Lord's resurrection (1 Cor.15:29).

For Jesus, Baptism is an absolute imperative for entry into the kingdom of Heaven. He assured Nicodemus "Unless a man is born again of water and the Spirit he cannot enter the kingdom of heaven (Jn.3:3-5)." Fr. Laport's mind was in a quandary for it had not been the practice of the Church to baptize the living on behalf of the dead. Notwithstanding that, he knew that Gina's children's souls would not rest unless they were placed into the hands of the Lord. Then he thought of the Baptism of Desire but Gina herself had only just been baptized and would have never thought of having her children baptized if they had been given a chance to see the light of day. There was no way of winning this argument. All the same, Fr. Laport thought that God would not mind if he put into action the teaching of St. Paul. Using 1 Corinthian chapter 15 verse 29 as the basis for his instruction, Fr. Laport instructed Gina and those who accompanied her, on the value and benefit of the Baptism of Desire and asked Gina whether it was her will, if these children had been given a chance to live and now that she was baptized, would she have wanted to baptize them. Gina answered in the affirmative. Thereby, Gina opened the door for the redemption of her children. Fr. Laport asked Harria and Evita to assist Gina in finding names for the twenty-six souls of her children. Gina had no problem naming the poor souls. It showed how much she missed them and longed to see them freed from their misery. Thus, Fr. Laport led Gina and her friends into prayer.

Fr. Laport: In the name of the Father and of the Son and of the Holy Spirit.

All: Amen

Fr. Laport: O God, Father Almighty, Lord and Giver of life. You are indeed God of the living, not God of the dead. Humankind is your work of art, created in Christ Jesus to live the good life as from the beginning he had meant humankind to live (Eph. 2:10). Humankind is your own image and likeness (Gen.1:26). You are the Father of all (Mat. 6:9). Your sons and daughters are transient beings in this world but destined to live forever with you in the world to come.

Mere mortals: you care for them. You made them inferior only to yourself; you crowned them with glory and honor. You appointed them rulers over everything you have made; you placed them over all creation (Ps. 8:5). Again and again, humankind has wandered away from your friendship. Yet you never cease to enter into a covenant with the people you claim as your own. Through Baptism in the name of the Blessed Trinity, humankind is continuously grafted as branches onto your Eternal Vine.

They are made your adopted children. In the Holy Eucharist you have established a new and everlasting covenant with your children (Mat. 26:28). Everyone who eats and drinks of your body and blood is given the pledge of eternal life (Jn. 6). In Confirmation, You strengthen the gifts and talents they received at Baptism. You ordain them: strong and perfect Christians and soldiers of your Son, Jesus Christ. At the celebration of your Son's glorious resurrection, your children renew the pledge of their initiation: they renounce the devil and all his works and earthly rewards to give themselves to you through the hands of Mary, your Mother. They reject sin in order to live as your children.

Egocentricity, greed, the lust for power and the tangibles of this life have corrupted and turned many hearts away from you. Headstrong and defiant and against all odds, many have violated your Fifth Commandment and have desecrated the lives of the unborn and the living. The words of your prophets have come true; "Fathers among you will eat their children, and children eat their fathers. I will inflict punishments on you and disperse what remains of you to the winds. (Eze. 5:10)." In all of this, O God, the victims are sufferers and they long to know your freedom.

The souls and spirits of the unborn and those used as human sacrifices languish. They long to see your face; they long for the portals of your kingdom. Through no fault of theirs, they are unable to enter on their own merit into your kingdom. They are unable to live in perfect peace with you, the angels and the saints. Your Son, O God, our Saviour Jesus Christ, has taught: "Unless a man is born through water and the Holy Spirit, he cannot enter the kingdom of God (Jn. 3.5)".

As your people Lord, we believe in the resurrection of the dead and the life of the world to come. Like Judas Maccabeus, despite the folly of men, we trust in your forgiveness, your mercy, love and compassion. We take full cognizance of the importance of offering sacrifice for our fallen ones. We believe that they will rise again when we cry to you on their behalf (2 Mc. 38-45). Your Apostle Paul assured the Corinthians: the souls of those who died before your Son's first coming shall live, if they, as believers, should receive Baptism on their behalf (1 Cor. 15:29). As a Christian community, we believe in the Baptism of Desire. Since it is the desire of those wounded and penitent souls that the fruits of their wombs see the light of your glory, therefore, O Lord, we bring to you the souls of the unborn and those offered up as human sacrifices. We believe you will redeem these helpless souls and welcome them among your holy people in heaven.

Therefore, O God, we bring to you the souls of all aborted ones and those offered up as human sacrifices in their infancy.

Penitential Rite

For these and for all our sins against humanity and against you, O God, we make David's Miserere our own.

All present pray the Psalm 50, (51) together and end with the following: Glory be to the Father and to the Son and to the Holy Spirit as it was in the beginning is now and will be forever. Amen.

Invocation of the Souls

In faith we call them by name to come into your presence:

Soul of: N............. Come to Jesus. Let Jesus wash you in his precious blood. Let Jesus direct you to the gates of heaven (3 times)

Baptism: The Rite

Rite of Committal of the Souls.

Thanksgiving

O God, Merciful Father and Lord of the living and the dead we thank you for your mercy, your compassion and your love, for hearing our prayers and opening the doors of your kingdom to these poor helpless souls who, through no fault of theirs, were left abandoned outside the gates of Paradise. Thank you Lord for hearing our prayers, Today, You have granted them the gift of eternal life and salvation with all your saints in heaven.

Shortly thereafter, Gina and her friends participated in the Mass of the day. At the end of Mass, Gina was a column of smiles. She approached Fr. Laport and said, "I saw all of them; they thanked me. They were all happy and smiling; all of them were wearing white gowns. They told me they're okay. There is no need to worry."

However, even though the waters had receded thus far, it was still only the tip of the iceberg. Gina's nightmare was still far from seeing its end. Gina and her friends were at prayer on the night following the Baptism of her children when she experienced an astral protection. She was overpowered by the spirit of someone called Julia. Without warning, Gina drifted from the prayers and Harria and Evita heard her babbling as if in an argument with someone. When confronted by Harria, the voice shouted back at her, "I'm Julia. I will kill you! I will kill Evita and that damn priest, I will kill him too! He's destroyed my angels and you all have aided and abetted with him. Gina will pay for that. She is nothing but an infidel wretch." Then, like a whirlwind, Gina's body went spiralling through the air. Again and again, Julia lifted Gina and slammed her against the wall as if she were just a flimsy twig. Harria and Evita covered their faces. Their throats were so constricted by fear that even if they wanted to cry out for help, they were unable to utter any syllables. So frightened were they that they temporarily forgot they were at prayer. The poor girls' nerves were so rattled that they were not sure whether or not they were to continue the prayers after all had quieted down. Before leaving though, Julia assured them she would be back.

For the first time in all of this drama, Harria and Evita understood exactly what Fr. Laport had been saying to them: "The journey will be long: let us take it one step at a time." At the next prayer session with Fr. Laport, Gina showed great signs of progress but Fr. Laport would not be fooled. He'd never forget his first experience in Solfatara Town. No! That was always fresh in his mind. This day in question, Fr. Laport took full authority over all the spirits who crowded Gina's life. He demanded that they depart from her life and from the room where Father, Gina and her two friends had gathered. He commanded them to cede their places to the Archangels and angels and the Blessed Virgin Mary. Gina's body jolted backwards and forward for a while to show that the spirits were not in conformity with Father's demand. Nevertheless, they were given no option other than to leave. They complied for the duration of the session.

Little did Fr. Laport know what awaited him. He never thought that Gina's revelations would one day draw tears from his heart. However they did, when he learnt that some men of the cloth were part and parcel and had, in some way, contributed to Gina's torments. The weight was much too much for Fr. Laport to carry alone at that point. At Gina's request, Bishop Lawrence was summoned to hear this tragic story with his own ears. The agony which enveloped the hearts of Bishop Lawrence and Fr. Laport in the presence of Gina's friends was, by far, beyond the power of words. Thankfully, Fr. Gozobeau, an exorcist, was in Helen Island for a visit. Bishop Lawrence had recognized then that Gina's case had taken a toll on already fragile Fr. Laport. He directed the case to Fr. Gozobeau for ongoing deliverance. Again, Fr. Gozobeau reiterated the words of Fr. Laport, "In some instances, a case as severe as Gina's could take as long as ten years minimum to see and experience a full recovery and redemption.

Evil has no ethnicity. It has no professional bias. It's easily accommodated in every social stratum. It is cultureless.

It was Friday morning. Gina, Harria and Evita arrived to be prayed with. It was the day when the official Prayer of Exorcism of the Catholic Church was scheduled to be prayed over Gina. The prayer team and all others involved in the process were well informed and briefed. Gina was deliberately left in the dark for fear that the spirits would intercept the process by keeping her away.

The group gathered before the Blessed Sacrament in a small reserved chapel and, after an extended examination of conscience, the chapel was sealed and all demons and spirit were commanded in the name of Jesus to depart and cede their place to Jesus, the angels, the saints and the Blessed Virgin Mary. Gina was then asked to kneel. She willingly obeyed. Fr. Laport, armed with his purple stole, a crucifix; holy water and exorcism prayer proceeded to pray over Gina. Towards the end of the prayer, Gina's body gradually started vibrating and climbed to a crescendo. It reached fever pitch. She broke into a sweat. Her body writhed from side to side; her eyes were almost out of their sockets when suddenly something like three columns of smoke was emitted from her body. Then she begged, "Please, let me go to the washroom. Please let me go. I will mess on the floor if I do not go." Fr. Laport hesitated for a while. He thought it was only a gimmick on the part of the spirit; but no, it was not. Something was coming out of Gina's loins. Harria accompanied her to the washroom. She'd passed something that looked like a slime ball. Gina returned to the chapel accompanied by Harria and resumed her kneeling position but within seconds, she begged again to return to the washroom. Her pains were too much to endure. Harria accompanied her. This time it was pieces of twigs from the cotton wood tree that were coming out of her loins. Harria assisted her in pulling them out. Gosh! The sight of Harria's face told the true story of the condition of her stomach. After the two visits to the washroom, all went well until Fr. Laport had completed the prayer of exorcism.

At the end of this episode, Gina showed tremendous signs of improvement. She was lucid, chatty and uninhibited by any spirits. In fact, she claimed a weight had been lifted from her shoulder and from within her body itself. She felt a new lease on life. Harria and Evita shouted, "Praise the Lord!" From then onward, Gina's heart and mouth were like open culverts. She stared Harria in the face and told her candidly of the deadly weapon Gobolda had placed in her hands to eliminate her. It's a weapon that has never yet been detected by any criminal investigator; plus, the cause of death had never yet been determined by any pathologist.

Gina told of her internal struggles when such a weapon was placed into her hands but her conscience did not permit her to use it for she knew deep down in her heart that Harria was her strength and the only human hope she had to see her deliverance through. She further confessed openly that many people had been killed by such means both at *black masses* and under normal circumstances. In the midst of Gina's confession, her cell buzzed.

Fr. Laport permitted her to answer. He wanted to know if the spirits were still in hot pursuit of Gina. He also wanted confirmation of what Gina had experienced during the prayer of exorcism. In fact it was. When Gina answered the call, she was told that three members of the cult had just moments earlier mysteriously died one after the other. Gina felt deep within her that the day of deliverance had come. Did she feel any sense of guilt? No! Gina was now free. In fact that was what Fr. Laport, Harria and Evita hoped for – Gina's total deliverance. However, Fr. Laport should have learnt from his

Solfatara experience that, in the world of witchcraft assignments, there are always backups and replacements. There is never a shortage of trafficking people waiting to enter the body of their victims.

Gina returned home that day and experienced a lull for a while. Just then the Lenten season was quickly approaching and there was talk of preparing Gina for the Sacraments of Confirmation and the Holy Eucharist. In the process of preparing Gina for the same, the backups and replacements made their debut and they physically manhandled Harria, Evita and Gina. The backups and replacements made no bones about it. They did not want Gina to receive the Holy Eucharist and the Sacrament of Confirmation. Every effort Harria and Evita made at instructing Gina was met with very stiff resistance. Their books and teaching materials were ripped from their hands and thrown helter-skelter. Every weekend Gina was sick, almost to the point of death. In such a condition, attending Mass or religious education classes was totally out of the equation. By the third Sunday in Lent, that was the third Sunday of the month of March, members of the cult were scheduled to commence their preparations for their triennium witches' conference and *black mass* celebrations in Helen Island.

On the third Sunday of Lent, their ritual was due to start at twelve midnight and conclude before two o' clock in the morning. On the second night, the meeting was scheduled for ten o' clock in the night to two o'clock in the morning. For one who is naïve, Gina's total recovery that weekend would have been nothing short of a miracle. No! It was not a miracle at all. It may have only been a partial deliverance. Total deliverance was still a long way off.

The backups and replacements had propped up her body and were preparing her for the occasion. She repeatedly told Harria and Evita that she was the key. Everything was about her. She told the girls that it was mandatory for her to be at all of the preparation meetings. The backups and replacements gave Gina strict instructions. They did not want her to receive first her Holy Communion or Confirmation. The reception of the sacraments would place a serious indictment on their efforts to reach her and to maintain their stronghold on her. Thankfully Harria and Evita would have none of that. They were just as determined as flint to protect Gina. By then, their efforts were frustrating the backups and replacements. Many times, they had come to carry Gina away but their presence and prayers would not permit them to.

Much to the horror of Harria and Evita, almost in a spontaneous refrain of choruses, the backups and replacements screamed out: "Harria, in Jesus' name, the only thing I can do right now is give up, give up to the demands of Gobolda! In Jesus' name I don't want to. In Jesus' name but it looks like that's the only way out in Jesus' name. I don't know where I am, in Jesus' name." At one time it sounded like Gina's voice, at another time, like the voice of a total stranger. In the interim, her body and mind vacillated and the struggle between the backups and replacements against Harria and Evita for control over Gina was on the verge of being a physical tussle but Harria would not fight. Prayer was her defence; prayer was her shield; her faith was her protection.

Harria and Evita maintained their hold over Gina that Sunday night. Come Monday, Harria and Evita were too weak to keep vigil with Gina. By Tuesday morning, Gina was in the den of the witches. Gina found herself in a windowless room with no lights and the door securely locked. She sent Harria a text message to say she had been locked up in isolation and that her pubic region had been shaved, unknown to her. From all indications it looked as if Gina was being prepared for sacrifice. Once again, Harria panicked; she needed help. She called Fr. Laport to the rescue and told him the story. He recommended: "Pray the Rosary of Liberation." Meanwhile, Father prayed the deliverance prayer and invited his prayer team to do the same around the clock.

While the prayers were in progress, Gina's telephone conversation with Harria was intercepted. A text message was sent. It read as follows: "You are losers! We have her now! All communication will cease as of now." Then all communication links between Gina and Harria were severed until later that day. At that point, Harria went berserk. Her hair was on end. Trying as hard as she could to restrain herself, her body quivered under the weight of her anxiety and trepidation. Thoughts of what would happen to Gina burned like fire in her mind and in her bones. Harria thought then that Gina would never be seen alive again. She held on to her chest and, at that point, it was evident that her heart was heavier than her head.

Nervousness had placed Evita in a quandary. She was worried for the safety of Gina but she was equally worried because she had seen the toll that Gina's disappearance had taken on Harria. It was taking place right before her eyes. While Evita's lips were silent, her hands spoke with abundant clarity: they were over her head, then placed over her lips, next over her ears and finally over her eyes. Simultaneously, her feet danced to the rhythm of fear and anguish. The unspoken lyrics were: 'I do not want to know anymore; I'll be silent forever. I want to hear no more and see no more.' The warning signs were there but they were long in coming. Tears streamed from Harria's eyes like broken culverts and then she regained her voice.

Harria screamed! "Father, in all honesty, I'm tired. I just feel like giving up. We have not slept properly for a little over a month now. Only last night, we took a break but we will do what we must. The spirits do not manifest for you like they do for us. Father, you just don't know. Whenever we pray with Gina alone, we are always under attack. Our books, our rosaries, everything is thrown helter-shelter. Many times, the spirits grab Evita and me by the throat. They have not choked us yet; it's a miracle. Sometimes, they literally push us against the wall. They have never manifested in your presence except to put Gina to sleep whenever you question her. But we will persevere. We just want it over."

Fr. Laport's heart went out to Harria and Evita. His only words of consolation at that point were: "It will at one point; God is our refuge and strength. In him all things work together for good for all who trust in him." These few words of consolation seemed to go a long way. They helped restore some measure of hope and confidence in Harria and Evita. Gradually, their tears ceased and their spirits were lifted. Like unwavering flames, their faith was rekindled and their cares were once again taken to the Lord in prayer. Fr. Laport looked at Harria and Evita with admiration. He shook his head. He just could not fathom the strength of these two young women. For his own good he told himself: 'Their strength is rooted in their faith and when God grants Gina total deliverance, it will not be through my efforts but because of the faith and resilience of these two very loving and humble ladies. Their prayers, in small measures, were always answered. Slowly but surely, God was opening a way for them through the turbulent waters.'

By mid-morning Gina had made a daring escape from the north of Féliciteville where she had been held in anticipation of whatever was to be her lot. She arrived in Stone Town, shaking like leaf on a windy day. She was out of her wits. The backup and replacement spirits were in hot pursuit. As soon as she stepped into the house, they took control of her with a determination to keep full control over her. In their effort to do so, they put up a nasty fight with Harria and Evita. Pretending that they were Gina, they kept on shouting, "In Jesus' name, the time has come, and I must go back to Rose Town. I must go back to the jungles of South America. That's where I belong. In Jesus' name, I must run away. If only you had understood, you would not tell me to be patient again. I want to kill myself. Let me go, in Jesus' name.' Gina went on and on and on. Harria and Evita looked on helplessly but indeed they were not, for they prayed all the while until Gina's body sank beneath the weight of her exhaustion. She'd crumbled onto the floor like a pile of dirty laundry and went into a deep sleep. Harria and Evita relished the hours that Gina slept. The atmosphere then was peaceful and it lent itself to an atmosphere of prayer and reflection. The girls took full advantage of the silence. They prayed ceaselessly for Gina all the while.

When Gina woke up, her eyes were glazed; they were hardened like marbles. She fixed her eyes into Harria's eyes and said, "I hope you know that, as Jesus Christ was sacrificed for the whole world, then it is Gina who must be sacrificed for the whole cult world." It was then that Harria and Evita realized it was not Gina who had been speaking all the while. It was the backup and replacement spirits. With their heads nudged forward and their eyes fully dilated, they looked at each other for a while as if to say: "Why are those spirits so insubordinate? Why won't they just give up?" At the end of their monologue, the spirits dared Harria and Evita to take Gina to a priest for Confirmation and the Holy Eucharist. If they dared, they would be killed but Harria and Evita never answered. By then, they were used to the threats of the spirits. They simply continued to bind the spirits and cast them out in the name of Jesus until they were either silenced or had departed to return at some other time.

Shortly thereafter, Harria turned to Fr. Laport and said, "You've been right all along. We are not dealing with flesh and blood. It looks like our battle will be for a long while still." Fr. Laport cleared his throat and said, "Wisdom has taught many before us that deliverance from the cult is always an uphill battle and its minimum duration can sometimes be ten years. The three of us can't continue this battle alone. We need the help of someone to journey with us." For once they realised they were in Nineveh and that Gina's teeth were still on edge because her fathers had eaten sour grapes and, until the cult world of her ancestors has crumbled, Gina's redemption, her salvation and her deliverance would be long in coming and at a tremendous cost.

Chapter Twelve

Jonah of Helen Island

In truth, this was no old wives' tale. It was more than just *Listwa* Time; nor was it just myths and legends. It was not another Anansi story. The ancestors were more than just artisans in the art of storytelling. They were teachers handing on to younger generations the oral traditions by which successive generations were able to safeguard themselves against evil in its various forms. But cultural myopia had blindfolded the youths from appreciating the collective wisdom of the elders and had left them, the youths, victims of social, religious and cultural dislocation.

Fr. Laport had to learn the hard way. First, he had to be a victim of colonialism before he could learn to appreciate the knowledge, experiences and collective wisdom of the oral tradition of his ancestors. Like many others, he had learned to mistrust and to mistreat such wisdom as mere myths, legends and dross in his youthful days. Never did he understand then that such precious moments which he considered only as *Listwa* Time were veritably quality enculturation *soirees*. These *soirees* were meant to prepare him and others for life; not just survival. These *soirees* gave him and his generation a peek into the thought patterns of his people. They were meant to help him and others understand the things that influenced the people's sense of judgement and behavioural patterns of their native peoples. These *soirees* started the ground work in Fr. Laport for his pastoral ministry: first in his ancestors' backyard and then, in his home environment and his pastoral territories. At one time, he had frowned on these foundations in preference for social acceptance at the expense of the very soul of his people. He was indeed a victim of cultural dislocation but he did not know it.

Culture is the soul of a people. It is the precise mold which God has used to fashion each nation, setting it apart distinctly different from others to mirror His multifaceted image and glory. To undermine any culture is to disfigure the people of God and the image of God in them.

For one who has been a victim of cultural dislocation, recovery is by far a hundred times more painful than a dislocated shoulder bone carried along in a sling. Recovery from cultural dislocation requires the retrofitting of a new mind, birthed in a culture and tradition that were once loathed in preference for a mindset which has always been foreign to one's very soul – one which has in more ways disfigured the victim's inner being and made him a charade, a charlatan in his own skin. Such attitudes subsequently have done untold damage to Fr. Laport's spirituality and ability to understand and to recognise the forces of evil at work right at his doorstep. In retrospection, Fr. Laport believes that such callous behaviour, on the part of those who misled so many generations to treat the wisdom of their ancestors with such scant disregard, has led many in the breaking of the Fourth Commandment, 'Honour your father and mother' (In matters of faith and morals). In so doing, they have deprived many of the longevity promised to those who honour their fathers and mothers. For Fr. Laport, Solfatara Town may have been an opportunity to reconsider his past and make good for the future.

If at all Solfatara Town was indeed Fr. Laport's 'Open University, the suburbs of Félicitéville, where he was born and spent his early years, were indeed the cradle where it all began. The foundation that was laid in Félicitéville was indeed a very robust foundation; one which endured the most rigorous of times and the colonial proverbial sledge wielded with ambidexterity and the determination to destroy all vestiges of lingering African belief systems in the Diaspora by way of reconfiguring the minds of the colonized. However, such attempts may never have achieved their intended objectives.

Fr. Laport's intimidation aroused by his encounters, exposures and experiences with the spirit world had nothing to do with his lack of faith. Fr. Laport has always believed that God created him a little less than himself and crowned him with power, authority and dominion over all the works of his hands (Ps. 8:5) and nothing could distract him from accepting such a noble gift. His real quandary was that he was schooled in a world disconnected to its own reality. Its self-imposed and imported teachers lived like neighbours in an apartment building. Yet, they never really knew their names or nationality but could only identify them by the colour of their skin.

Any attempts made by any of these neighbours to reveal their names and identity came with mistrust and deep-seated fear. Such was the case with Fr. Laport in Solfatara Town. He lived within a community where he heard his neighbours' voices but he never deciphered their language or even recognised their accent. He did not even know their pain and agony; yet they were all sons and daughters of fair 'Helen Island'; Solfatarians together. For them, he was called from among them to lead them out of bondage of all kinds to total freedom; yet he treated the enemies of their souls as myths and legends. Consequently, his failure to acknowledge such enemies in their varied forms of existence and manifestations, left him at a disadvantage at the beginning of his public priestly ministry.

Nonetheless, Fr. Laport believed that God had a very strange sense of humour. Even when one is most reluctant to sail to the destination God has in mind for him, God himself provided a whale to get him to the designated destination to which he was sent. Fr. Laport was of the firm conviction that he was a Jonah in the hands of God, only that his Nineveh seemed a lot larger than Jonah's and his message was taking much longer to sink in. Yet, for all it took, he was still willing to plod along until the kingdoms around him fall with

God's help and his place was secured not in the stomach of a whale but in the kingdom up above. If there is one thing that colonialism taught him, it is that appearances are not always the right gauge of human quality and that goes both ways: both in matters of culture and faith.

Chapter Thirteen

Desecrated Humans

The lust for power, wealth and fame has sullied the boudoirs of the virgin Helen Island and has tarnished her reputation and her character. Even her integrity has definitely been compromised. Her boudoirs have been converted into sanctuaries of Baphomet; their communion sacrifices, the flesh and blood of desecrated humans. Vows have been written on her walls, carved in scarlet letters and smoked into concealment so that the parade of charlatans may flourish undetected and these demons mimic the glory of saints while real saints are dismissed as shams. There, at the Altar of the Word, duplicity is praised and canonized. Right at the altar, witches and wizards are eulogized and saints are demonized. Power and fame are the gauges by which our world judges men and women worthy of the kingdom. There at the altar, virtue, grace and faith are often put to shame. Witches and wizards are clothed in all institutional garbs. Like wolves in sheep's clothing, they snarl undetected in the shepherds' hands, diminishing flocks of every breed. Such is the fate of honour, social recognition, the halls of fame and the nave of faith.

History repeats itself in successive generations. There are always those who stubbornly adhere to the principles of self-destruction while casting aspersions on those who preceded them. They change the faces of rites and rituals only to serve the same masters their ancestors served to arrive at the same destination. The old adage has it: *"Tig mò mé zonng'y la toujou."* Literally translated, "The ancestors have passed on but their descendants live on to perpetuate their misdeeds."

Many questions have been asked. Many speculations still vie for answers. The fate that sealed the demise of the Aztecs and Mayan peoples is still unanswered. It is believed that their practice of human sacrifice contributed much to their extinction as a people. If such is the veracity which upholds their narrative, then this must be acknowledged: their gods were the gods of self-destruction, not the God of life. Otherwise, they would not have been wiped out of existence.

Has the Western world in the twenty-first century learned anything from the fate of the Aztecs and Mayans? And if not, how much has western man come of age in this twenty-first century? If, in past generations, alliances with demons have contributed nothing to the peace and stability of man, why on earth has membership in cults become so rampant today and human sacrifices more prevalent than ever? Witches and wizards have infiltrated every possible human and religious institution; not one is exempt. All have come short of the Glory of God and the *faux pas* and misdeeds of past generations have done little to rearrange modern man's idiosyncrasies in pursuit of things that are all transient.

"In Turbulent Waters" is an insight of a short list of persons in Helen Island who, through their demonic affinity with Baphomet and his angels, have contributed nothing constructive to their families, their nation and religion as a whole. At the hands of man and the hands of the gods of heaven, their only lot has been pain, rejection, self-destruction and death. Satan lives to steal, to kill and destroy those who are sufficiently stupid and gullible to believe in his promises when the earth and its fullness is God's. The gullible and revengeful shall reap only what Satan has sown.

As with Gerald, Ma Fano, Bolo, Jablé, Carmen, Dada, Dubois, Patrick, Harold and Beth, Roland, Ma Claratine, Harrison, Ma Pépé and Poli and Ruffina, Julian, Jagkaribe and his wife, Elfita, Gobolda, Ziptapis, Pyonica, Manitus, Phillippa and Tyra, Hilton or Uzoboth, their lives and dubious activities have left a bitter legacy for their descendents for generations to come. Their children and children's children for many generations will repeat the words of the prophet Ezekiel: "The fathers ate sour grapes and the children's teeth are still on edge." Their victims will go forth to tell the story. Good always triumphs over evil! They, who have known the bitterness of evil, shall have no partnership with Satan and his angels, for he and his angels come only to steal, kill and to destroy! Nevertheless, good shall always triumph over evil (Jn. 10:10). Furthermore, God always fulfill His promise: good shall always triumph over evil!

Postscript

The ancestors, with their limited pedantic capacity, did all they possible could, to transmit, to successive generations the necessary social, cultural cum spiritual virtues and values that are inherent to a holistic way of life. Through the medium of *Listwa Time,* the forefathers did their utmost to divert their children's attention away from atheism and individualism. Their efforts were not spent in vain; God was present in every sense of the word. He was needed and He had a meaning and a reason for everything which contributed to the formation of character, the need for community and unity, the existence of the world and of humankind.

Faith played a formidable role in shaping the consciousness and conscience of many generations. The sacramental life of the Church played a pivotal role in preparing each person for their rightful contribution in the home, community and the world. The sense of community and unity then stood much taller than that of today's rampant individualism and pluralism, in today's world, where God appears to be less present and less needed; humankind is unwilling to accept God's explanation of both personal and social life (cf. G.S.5, 7).[2] Instead, we have become very pluralistic and permissive. God is readily trivialized and the commandments are deemed obsolete. Humanism and relativity are the norms of the day; arrogance is considered a blessing, while the prosperity of evildoers enhances the credibility of such social, cultural and spiritual deficiencies until the day of reckoning comes, leaving them like stubble (Mal. 3:13-20).

---

[2] Cf. Sacred Congregation for the Clergy General Catechetical Directory, The Incorporated Catholic Truth Society, London and Pell (Brighton) Ltd., Brighton, Sussex, England, 1973,§5

Despite humankind's quest for independence away from God, there is still a lurking hunger in the human soul for a center and for communion with a power other than themselves. There is still an element of helplessness within them to achieve their goals all on their own. The result is obvious: either persons create a god for themselves or they become disciples of Baphomet and his angels. The end result is always a disaster – self-destruction. According to Malachi, they will be left with "neither root nor stalk."

Humankind is created in the image and likeness of God. They are crowned with power, glory and splendour; they are lord over all of creation, and all things are set under their feet (Ps. 8:5). Only faith will empower humankind to harness all the resources and treasures God has already bestowed upon them. There is more divine power at work in man, in his human estate than there is in Baphomet and his angels. Besides, Baphomet is a liar from the beginning. He exists only to steal, to kill and to destroy. The Lord exists that all who believe in Him may have life in abundance (Jn.10:10). Therefore, recognizing that humankind is a mirror of God, that humankind is God's property, that their salvation has been bought and paid for with the currency of the blood of the Lamb Jesus Christ (1Pet. 1:19), humankind, should therefore make every effort to "Put God's amour on so as to be able to resist the devil's tactics … to put up any resistance when the worst happens, or have enough resources to hold your ground (Eph. 6:11, 17)."

The author, therefore, urges all his readers: "Do not be dismayed, not even in your darkest moments. Stay focused! Be faithful to the Lord and He will be faithful to you (2Tim. 2:13). He is the Way, the Truth and the Life (Jn. 14:6). Follow that way and you will find life. There is still hope. Be like Gina and her two friends. Put up a fight! Turn to the sentinels the Lord has placed at every junction where temptation awaits. Listen to them; they will help. "Put yourselves on the ways of long ago, enquire about the ancient paths: which was the good way? Take it then, and you will find rest (Jer. 6:16)."

The author further recommends the help of spiritual directors and the frequenting of the sacraments of the Church. For those who have already fallen into the snare of the devil, there is still hope through the ministry of repentance and exorcism. Visit your local bishop and he will direct you to the appointed exorcists in your respective diocese. Do not be afraid to trust in God. He is patiently awaiting your return home. Fr. Laport, through faith, has stood the worst of times and he believes that you can as well. With Jesus at your side, you can reach the place God has in mind for you (Heb. 3:7-19).

Bibliography

The Jerusalem Bible, London, Darton, Longman & Todd, 1966

The Roman Missal, English Translation According To The Third Edition, Catholic Truth Society, St. Pauls Publication, 2010.

General Catechetical Directory, Catholic Truth Society, publishers for the Holy See, London, England, 1973